The European Security and Defense Policy

NATO's Companion —or Competitor?

Robert E. Hunter

RAND

RAND *Europe*

NATIONAL DEFENSE RESEARCH INSTITUTE

The research described in this report was conducted jointly by RAND Europe and the International Security and Defense Policy Center of RAND's National Defense Research Institute, a federally funded research and development center supported by the Office of the Secretary of Defense, the Joint Staff, the unified commands, and the defense agencies under Contract DASW01-01-C-0004.

ISBN: 0-8330-3117-1

RAND is a nonprofit institution that helps improve policy and decisionmaking through research and analysis. RAND® is a registered trademark. RAND's publications do not necessarily reflect the opinions or policies of its research sponsors.

Cover designed by Stephen Bloodsworth

Published 2002 by RAND
1700 Main Street, P.O. Box 2138, Santa Monica, CA 90407-2138
1200 South Hayes Street, Arlington, VA 22202-5050
201 North Craig Street, Suite 102, Pittsburgh, PA 15213
RAND URL: http://www.rand.org/
To order RAND documents or to obtain additional information, contact Distribution Services: Telephone: (310) 451-7002; Fax: (310) 451-6915; Email: order@rand.org

Few issues have been more vexing to American policy analysts and political leaders than the emergence of the European Security and Defense Policy (ESDP) in the last two-thirds of the 1990s and continuing into the new century. The United States has long advocated the development of a European "pillar" within NATO—in essence the idea that a politically and economically strong Europe should contribute roughly equal military capacity as the United States to mutual security. But there have been two ideas embedded in the pillar concept—not only military strength, but also strength within NATO, not outside it.

The Europeans are critically important security partners of the United States. Almost no conceivable security task can be handled without their help, especially in and near Europe, but also well beyond it. Americans have long been concerned that European military weakness is harmful to NATO and to the United States, to say nothing of the Europeans themselves. Since the 1999 war with Serbia, most European leaders and analysts now acknowledge (sometimes grudgingly) that Europe's military capacity is too weak. For this reason the emergence of ESDP ought to be a welcome development to the United States. Perhaps the pillar will finally be erected.

But the ESDP process has turned out to be a bittersweet development. It has been fraught with political maneuvers that raise questions of whether ESDP will be within NATO or outside of it. The worst possible outcome from an American point of view has seemed possible—a continuation of European military weakness (as European defense budgets remain tiny) and a separation of Europe from NATO. This would mean a net decrease in American security because

NATO has proved a valuable instrument in the post–cold war era: The political-military structures and habits developed within NATO have been essential to military success in the Balkans and in the 1990–91 Gulf War.

This is a complicated subject. Politics, economics, national cultures, and numerous institutions are intertwined. The subject has become even more complex following the attack on the Pentagon and the World Trade Center on September 11, 2001, and the first-ever invocation of Article 5 of the Washington Treaty the following day.

It is hard for American observers (even for European ones) to get a firm grip on these developments and their implications. In this book, Robert Hunter provides the best chronicle yet of the emergence of ESDP and its shifting relationship to NATO. He is well placed to do so. From 1993–98 he was a direct participant in the unfolding story as the U.S. Ambassador to NATO, and he negotiated for the United States the basic arrangements between NATO and the Western European Union, then the custodian of ESDP. Since then, as senior advisor to the president of RAND, he has kept a watchful eye on ESDP and NATO.

Robert's is clearly an American perspective. But readers, both American and European, will benefit from both his assessment of the past and his recommendations for the way forward. They are aimed at both American and European policymakers. In fashioning his recommendations, Robert has taken careful account of European security interests and political concerns. This monograph was completed prior to September 11. Robert has included an Afterword to indicate in what ways the debate over ESDP has changed since then, what has not changed, and what should be done in the new circumstances to ensure that this European Union effort to forge a European pillar does, indeed, strengthen transatlantic relations.

Not all North American and European readers, including this one, will agree with every point contained herein. But all will come away with a better understanding of this complex subject and with workable policy ideas for the future.

James Thomson
President
RAND
September 2001

This study is the product of more than two years' research and writing as part of a wider National Defense Research Institute–financed project on overall U.S. engagement in European security and institutional arrangements across the Atlantic. It relies heavily on the author's background, which includes a doctoral dissertation at the London School of Economics (1969) on the origins of the Brussels Treaty—the forerunner of Western European Union[1] (WEU) and, hence, the European Security and Defence Policy (ESDP); responsibility for both NATO and European community affairs at the National Security Council (1977–79); and service as U.S. ambassador to NATO and representative of the United States to the WEU (1993–98), during which time the author played a key role in formulating U.S. policy toward the European pillar and negotiated for the United States new arrangements between NATO and WEU—as the then executive agent for what is now called the European Union's ESDP.

This study should be of interest to a wide audience, including those interested in the evolution of U.S.-European relations, especially in,

---

[1]The first post–World War II Western security institution was Western Union (WU), created in 1948; this was enlarged and renamed the Western European Union (WEU) in 1954. During 2000–01, the WEU was in the process of being absorbed within the European Union (EU). Regarding nonmilitary European integration, the first formal institution was the European Coal and Steel Community (ECSC) of 1951. Following negotiation of the Treaty of Rome in 1956, it was supplemented by the European Economic Community (EEC) and the European Atomic Energy Community (EURATOM). These became collectively referred to as the European Communities, or European Community (EC). In 1992, the three institutions were integrated and renamed the European Union.

but not limited to, the security field; the development of institutional relationships; and key choices that lie ahead regarding U.S.-European relations. For students of process and Atlantic Alliance history, this study lays out the development of what NATO has called the European Security and Defense Identity and what the European Union calls ESDP. For policymakers—on both sides of the Atlantic—this study provides an essential background for understanding how security issues between NATO and the European Union are being raised for the early part of the 21st century. These include the new circumstances following the terrorist attacks in New York, Washington, and Pennsylvania on September 11, 2001. For policymakers, this study also provides guidelines for helping to ensure that the creation of ESDP—including a new European rapid reaction force—can strengthen the Atlantic Alliance overall, and especially relations with the United States. The study seeks to be comprehensive—as befits any effort to delve deeply into the reality of policy discussion and decision—and includes analysis of burden sharing, influence within the alliance, the role of various allies and the two basic institutions, and the ways in which both institutions can and should develop a relationship (quite different from the cold war years) that can be mutually beneficial.

This research was conducted jointly by RAND Europe and the International Security and Defense Policy Center of RAND's National Defense Research Institute, a federally funded research and development center sponsored by the Office of the Secretary of Defense, the Joint Staff, the unified commands, and the defense agencies.

CONTENTS

TABLES

BACKGROUND

Beginning in 1993, the United States began giving strong support to the development of a vigorous "European pillar" within the Atlantic Alliance. In June 1996, NATO and the WEU negotiated framework agreements that served as the basis for creating this European pillar within the alliance. This pillar would potentially draw upon NATO military capabilities that could be "separable from but not separate from" the alliance. The WEU would be permitted to make use of certain NATO assets—including staff officers, military equipment not available to the WEU states, the Deputy Supreme Allied Commander Europe, and NATO's new Combined Joint Task Force (CJTF) headquarters. These would be available to help the WEU undertake so-called Petersberg Tasks, ranging from humanitarian missions to peacemaking, in circumstances when NATO as a whole—in effect, the United States—chose not to be involved.

Two years later, French President Chirac and British Prime Minister Blair took a step further, declaring that the European Security and Defense Policy should also have the capacity for "autonomous" action. And at the end of 1999, the European Union states agreed to create a Headline Goal Task Force—popularly called "the European rapid reaction force"—that would be ready, from 2003 onward, to undertake some of the Petersberg Tasks.

For the last several years, there has been intense debate across the Atlantic about the relationship between NATO and the European Union, in regard to the latter's ESDP; about how ESDP should function—what it should do and, equally important, what tasks it should leave to NATO; about the proper role for the Headline Goal Task Force; about the level of European defense spending and the equipment that a European force should "duplicate" rather than draw from NATO; and—beneath the surface of the debate—the relative distribution of political influence, both within Europe and between the United States and its European allies.

As ESDP has developed, at least 11 separate purposes have emerged as central:

- Move the process of European integration forward.

- Lay the basis for the EU's eventually having a truly functioning "European" foreign policy.

- Provide one framework for adjusting relative political influence within the European Union.

- Enable the Europeans to have an added insurance policy so that they could act with some military force if NATO (meaning, in practice, the United States) chose not to be engaged.[2]

- Address the constant refrain from the United States about "burden sharing" within the alliance.

- Provide added political incentive for modernizing European military forces and ensuring that, to the degree possible, they remain interoperable with more rapidly modernizing U.S. military forces.

- Give the Europeans some more say in decisions reached within NATO.

- Give European governments a greater say regarding a legal mandate for military action.

---

[2]By common agreement, NATO retains responsibility for the collective defense of the alliance, as covered by Article 5 of the Treaty of Washington. But regarding the tasks that the EU might undertake under the Petersberg Tasks, there is no formal separation—or division of labor—between what operations the EU could undertake as opposed to those that NATO could undertake. However, as part of the understanding within the alliance that there should be "one NATO, not two" is the implication that, at some level of military action, an EU operation could have to engage NATO with its much more extensive and robust capabilities.

- Buttress the process of EU enlargement into Central Europe.

- Spur the consolidation of European armaments industries, provide some added demand for military equipment, and create a political framework for competing and cooperating with their American counterparts.

- Tackle the long-standing question of the relative distribution of influence within the broader Atlantic Alliance.

U.S. ASSESSMENT

The United States should accept and support most if not all of these ESDP goals. Since the 1940s, the United States has promoted European integration. It clearly welcomes efforts that will reduce recurrent European fears that the United States will "decouple" its security from Europe's. It welcomes incentives to increase European defense spending, especially to demonstrate adequate burden sharing within the alliance and to help European militaries be interoperable with U.S. forces.

The United States should also welcome the development of a Headline Goal Task Force that focuses on development of military capabilities that can also contribute to NATO. The United States should welcome development of an ESDP and a Common Foreign and Security Policy (CFSP) that can lead Europe to play a more active role beyond the European continent. The United States should also welcome a European capability for crisis management, especially civilian aspects, and even the use of military force in situations that fall below the threshold where NATO—meaning, in practice, the United States—would need to become engaged.

ESDP also raises some issues of serious concern for the United States that need to be resolved to ensure that NATO and EU actions through ESDP will be compatible with one another, that they will work toward the same basic objectives, and that transatlantic security and political relations will be strengthened, not weakened, by the development of ESDP. Notable are the following:

- ESDP may stimulate greater European defense spending, but that spending might go primarily to purchase capabilities that NATO already has in abundance; or it could be wasteful in terms of efficient use of scarce resources; or it could stimulate European efforts to close or restrict arms markets to competition from outside, including the United States.

- By contrast, ESDP could lead some allies to believe that they can meet the military requirements of the Headline Goal Task Force without facing the more expensive demands of NATO force modernization, especially NATO's Defense Capabilities Initiative (DCI), at a time of rapid U.S. modernization, thereby risking the "hollowing out" of alliance military capabilities.

- ESDP could, whether intended or not, cause competition with NATO's structures and processes.

- Differences regarding planning have special significance. First, potentially having more than one place where operational planning takes place could produce different outcomes that would complicate any situation in which the EU, acting through ESDP, had to hand over responsibility to NATO, or where NATO had to decide what forces it could usefully transfer to an ESDP operation without prejudicing its own ability to act. A compromise could be the use of "national" headquarters (Britain or France) for only some relatively low-level operations or for operations in some specific areas (such as parts of Africa) where there would be a low probability of NATO engagement, provided this planning were fully transparent to NATO. Second, if defense planning (i.e., determining force structure over time) were bifurcated, inconsistencies, incompatibilities, and inefficiencies could become worse.

- The demands of internal political cohesion within the EU could make it difficult to resolve the issue of full participation by non-EU NATO members—notably Turkey—thus risking a split in allied cohesion.

- Political impetus to make CFSP and ESDP effective could lead to a "European caucus" within NATO which, if truly pursued to meet the provisions of the Consolidated Version of the Treaty on European Union, could impair the capabilities of the North Atlantic Council and could tend to produce "least common denominator" outcomes.

- The process of relating crisis management to the use of force could complicate the issue of determining just how NATO would gain what the United States sees, but not all European allies see, as a necessary right of first refusal—i.e., when it would be determined that NATO as a whole is not prepared to be engaged.[3]

- European rhetoric about ESDP could become so exaggerated that some U.S. observers would (erroneously) believe that the EU, through ESDP, could take over more of the common burdens, and reduce those falling on U.S. shoulders, than would in fact be the case.

- Differences in the way in which the purposes of ESDP are characterized by different European states and political leaders could continue to sow confusion in the United States—especially risking that the EU, acting through ESDP, would be seen as a potential competitor for NATO.

- A reverse problem could arise if a "division of labor" developed between EU/ESDP and NATO (especially along the lines of concentration on relatively high and low military technologies). This "division of labor" could produce an implicit fracture in the assumption that providing security in Europe is a common good to be pursued by all allies. At the same time, what the United States is prepared to do in allied Balkan operations would have a significant impact on perceptions of the overall U.S. commitment to engage in "real life" NATO activities containing some degree of risk. In 2001, expressed U.S. doubts about putting troops at risk in a NATO force for Macedonia raised some concerns among other allies. However, some limited "division of labor" could be acceptable in crises or other challenges beyond Europe, where the United States would not want to be engaged, nor the allies require it. This is especially true in parts of Africa.

- The issue of the relative balance of influence between the United States and some or all European states could become sufficiently

---

[3]It may be unlikely that all the European allies would accept that NATO should have the right of first refusal—the assignment of responsibility being a matter for consultation in each instance. But as a practical matter, there seems to be no value for ESDP, and certainly not for NATO, in the EU's insisting that it might "go it alone" militarily when NATO would be prepared to take the lead.

bound up with the structure and conduct of ESDP that crucial elements could be lost, such as the principles of common commitment by all allies to European security, broad risk sharing, and subordination of such issues as the balance of political influence to more-practical matters of getting the European security job done.

PRACTICAL STEPS

Nevertheless, on balance, for the United States the role of ESDP is strongly positive, *provided* that remaining problems can be resolved:

"NATO First"

There needs to be wholehearted, unambiguous European adherence to the principle that the Headline Goal Task Force will act only "where NATO as a whole is not engaged." Many Europeans will resist the notion that this implies "NATO first":[4] But as a practical matter, it is important for preserving cohesion of the Alliance.

Shared Risks/No Division of Labor

There needs to be reaffirmation of the cardinal NATO principle that risks are to be shared by all allies and that there must not emerge, formally or informally, a "division of labor" between NATO and EU/ESDP, except in relatively marginal operations outside of Europe.

Furthermore, how the Bush administration develops policies toward the Balkans and peacekeeping/peacemaking roles for U.S. forces, in general, cannot be separated from its hopes for an ESDP that is compatible with its hopes for NATO. Any U.S. reluctance to share such risks and tasks, especially in the Balkans, would be incompatible with an effort to keep ESDP simply as a second-choice option for dealing with crisis and conflict in Europe.

---

[4] Helsinki European Council, *Presidency Conclusions*, December 10–11, 1999.

Cooperative Planning

Approaches to operational planning must not put NATO and EU/ESDP at loggerheads. In parallel, methods of defense planning must be mutually compatible, preferably with a single set of processes. Cooperation should include shared contingency planning, conducted by the Supreme Headquarters, Allied Powers Europe (SHAPE) Combined Joint Planning Staff, with full participation by the EU Military Staff. There should be only one methodology for command, control, communications, and intelligence (C^3I). Also, the EU should predesignate NATO's Deputy Supreme Allied Commander, Europe (SACEUR) as force generator, strategic coordinator, and operational commander for all ESDP missions.

Defense Spending and Capabilities

European governments need to commit themselves to keep defense spending up or, where it is falling, to stop the slide (Germany is currently the highest priority). Emphasis needs to be put on outputs, on capabilities relevant to well-analyzed future requirements, and on interoperability. Even within existing budgets, efforts to promote the Defense Capabilities Initiative must not slacken. At the very least, priorities within the DCI should emphasize core NATO requirements, extending to doctrine, training, and style of operations as well as to force structure and equipment. The European allies should avoid duplicating those NATO assets that would be available to the EU (through the ESDP) where these divert defense moneys away from other critical areas; European development of the A400M transport aircraft is the most egregious current example. But if the United States wants ESDP to avoid "unnecessary duplication," it must reassure the Europeans that NATO would release NATO assets, including U.S. equipment operated by U.S. service members, especially large transport aircraft.

Interoperability

The EU under ESDP needs to concentrate its force modernization on interoperability with NATO, especially within the DCI. It is critical that two levels of interoperability do not develop—one for the United States and a handful of key European allies (notably the United

Kingdom), and one for the rest: This would be a sure recipe for bifurcation, an implicit if not explicit division of labor among alliance tasks, and a corrosion of the spirit of cohesion that has been an alliance hallmark. In addition to shared responsibility to meet DCI goals, the United States needs to share high technology with allies—this is a major priority.

NATO Crisis Management

NATO needs to develop means for being linked to a crisis management mechanism, paralleling the CFSP and ESDP. There must also be prior agreement that discussion and dialogue between NATO and the EU will be deep, wide, continuous, and effective at all stages of any emerging crisis that could affect both bodies.

Political Focus: EU/ESDP and NATO

There is a premium on the rapid completion of basic ESDP and CFSP institution building, so that attention can begin moving away from the current intense focus on developing bureaucratic structures related to ESDP and toward the what, the how, and the how much real resources of European security.

Political and Strategic Dialogues

There needs to be solid, sustained political and military dialogue between the EU—through ESDP/CFSP—and NATO and between national governments and parliaments. This is especially true regarding the U.S. Congress. In particular, the transatlantic dialogue on "burden sharing" has often been poisoned by different definitions of the term: with the United States' focusing almost exclusively on military activity; and with the Europeans' demanding credit for nonmilitary contributions to a broader definition of "security." A thoughtful dialogue across the Atlantic is essential if burden sharing is not to become an increasing irritant in transatlantic relations.

Managing Rhetoric and Ambition

The European Union needs to exercise restraint—and provide clarity—in its rhetoric about what ESDP is and what it is not, especially in dealing with the United States and, more particularly, the U.S. Congress. There is a risk that inflated declarations of ESDP aspirations will be taken for reality, where that is not justified; alternatively, shortfalls in ESDP, relative to declared aspirations, can intensify U.S. congressional criticism that the Europeans are not pulling their weight. It is especially important that those members of the EU that care most about preserving the vitality and cohesion of the transatlantic relationship, as well as NATO's primacy, ensure that "autonomy" for EU decision and action through ESDP not become the central focus of the European pillar; this aspiration needs to be kept in perspective in relation to other European security goals. A parallel risk is that some members of the U.S. Congress will read into excessive ESDP rhetoric more of a challenge to NATO's primacy than any European leader intends, thus deepening suspicions.

The U.S. government also needs to speak with as much of "one voice" as is possible for Washington. Certainly key officials should present U.S. support and aspirations for ESDP and concerns about its development clearly and consistently. President Bush's leadership on this issue needs to be followed throughout the bureaucracy. The administration must also help ensure that debate on Capitol Hill centers on the facts of ESDP, not misperceptions about it.

Defense-Cooperation "Code of Conduct"

An effective transatlantic dialogue and a NATO-EU defense-cooperation code of conduct need to be developed for governments and industry. This code should focus on five principles: (1) keep U.S. and European arms markets open to each other; (2) share as much defense high technology within the alliance as possible; (3) develop common standards and measures for protecting shared technologies; (4) emphasize interoperability within transatlantic defense cooperation; and (5) focus on at least ensuring "open architecture"—i.e., the design of new technologies to be compatible with other allies' military equipment—to minimize the risks of a technologically two-tiered alliance. In time, there should be common NATO and

EU/ESDP acquisition planning to help harmonize requirements and responses.

Uses of Military Power

There needs to be a continuing, broad strategic dialogue within NATO about the purposes of military capabilities and defense spending. For both NATO and EU/ESDP, building, training, sustaining, and exercising military forces must be clearly related to what these forces are expected, at some point, to do. For democracies to continue spending significant funds on defense—and potentially to risk the lives of young men and women in military combat—strategic analysis, political vision, and dialogue among nations and institutions are indispensable.

Leadership

Finally, these recommendations for defusing the disagreements within the alliance about ESDP need to be followed at the highest levels of government until key differences are resolved, so that there is a productive, mutually reinforcing relationship between NATO and EU/ESDP, even if not always tension-free. Allied and EU leaders should focus on six key "cooperations" between NATO and the European Union: (1) operational planning, (2) contingency planning, (3) defense and capabilities planning, (4) acquisition planning and a transatlantic defense-cooperation code of conduct, (5) North Atlantic Council–Political and Security Committee interaction that ideally also engages the Euro-Atlantic Partnership Council, and (6) joint crisis management.

"Getting ESDP right" is a necessary goal on its own. That should be gained with sufficient leadership, understanding, and commitment on both sides of the Atlantic. But it is also essential for the allies to "get right" other critical disagreements on such matters as threats to allied territories from beyond Europe, missile defenses, defense investments by European allies, the risk of a "hollowed out" NATO, NATO enlargement, engaging Russia, stability in the Balkans, and the long-term perspectives both of European security and of overall U.S. relations with Europe, including the European Union.

Finally, resolving current issues in NATO–EU/ESDP relations is, at least for the near and medium term, more about political will and tactics than about long-term goals and strategy. On this effort, three points stand out:

- The ESDI-ESDP issue should not be allowed to divide the United States and European allies in any fundamental way.

- Getting ESDP right should be high on the current transatlantic agenda and for political action by leaders on both sides of the Atlantic.

- There is no apparent reason why serious efforts by U.S. and EU leaders should not produce the desired results: a mutually reinforcing relationship between the EU (acting through ESDP) and NATO that works for all and for overall security in the transatlantic region.

ACKNOWLEDGMENTS

I wish to acknowledge and thank all those who were instrumental either in informing the work that follows or in helping to bring it to fruition. I especially thank RAND's leadership—President James Thomson (also for his generous Foreword), Michael Rich, Jeff Isaacson, and Stuart Johnson for making it possible for me to conduct this research and write the monograph. Stephen Larrabee, Chair in European Security at RAND, read the manuscript, as did Holger Pfeiffer, NATO Deputy Assistant Secretary General, Defence Planning and Operations, and their comments were insightful and invaluable. In the course of my research, I spoke with numerous people, including some at NATO and the European Union. Although I risk leaving some out, let me thank Lord George Robertson, NATO Secretary General; General Joseph Ralston, Supreme Allied Commander Europe; General Rupert Smith, Deputy Supreme Allied Commander Europe; General Klaus Naumann (ret.), former Chairman, NATO Military Committee; VADM Norman Ray (ret.), former Vice Chairman, NATO Military Committee; Robert Hall and Clarence Juhl, U.S. Mission to NATO; Ambassador Gunter Burghardt, Head of the Delegation of the European Commission to the United States; Fraser Cameron, Deputy Head of the commission delegation; Jonathan Davidson of the delegation; European Union officials, including Lodewijk Briet, the advisor responsible for specific CFSP matters in the EU External Relations Directorate-General and Lars-Eric Lundin, Directorate A (CFSP), EU External Relations Directorate-General; James Elles, MEP, European Parliament; and many others.

Much of the material in this monograph is derived from nearly four decades' work on issues related to NATO, WEU, and the European pillar of the alliance, beginning with graduate studies at the London School of Economics, which culminated in a doctoral dissertation on the origins of Western Union; and carrying through four and a half years as U.S. ambassador to NATO (July 1993–January 1998), during which time I also represented the United States to the Western European Union. This included the period in which NATO and the WEU negotiated the basic agreements that have led to today's NATO-EU relationship and the development of both ESDI and ESDP. During that period, I had the incomparable advantage of being supported by a superb team of U.S. officials, especially at the U.S. Mission to NATO—from the Defense Department (military and civilian), the State Department, the United States Information Agency, and the Federal Emergency Management Agency. This team played a decisive role in creating the "new NATO" and, with it, the development of the European pillar within NATO.

My thanks also to RAND's Risha Henneman, who has shepherded this monograph through to completion. And—most of all—my deep appreciation to my wife, Shireen Hunter, for her wise counsel, encouragement, and support throughout this project.

While so many people contributed to the ideas contained in this monograph, the responsibility for judgments, conclusions—and errors—is mine.

Chapter One

BACKGROUND

For the past several years, the United States, Canada, their European allies, and other countries belonging to the European Union (EU)[1] have resumed a long-standing debate about the relationship between the North Atlantic Treaty Organization (NATO) as a whole and a European defense "pillar" of the Western alliance. Historically, this debate has always had several strands: Most prominent have been the characteristics and pace of the development of European integration, chiefly enshrined in the European Union; the management of security within the West—until 1991 focusing on the Soviet Union and now oriented more broadly; the sharing of common transatlantic defense burdens among the various countries of Western Europe and North America; and the distribution of political influence, both within the two key institutions—NATO and the EU—and in general between the United States and its partners.

In about 1993, the latest round of debate began in earnest, with two notable developments: widespread recognition that NATO still retained a purpose following the end of the cold war—to paraphrase

---

[1]The first post–World War II Western security institution was Western Union (WU), created in 1948; this was enlarged and renamed the Western European Union (WEU) in 1954. During 2000–2001, the WEU was in the process of being absorbed within the European Union (EU). Regarding nonmilitary European integration, the first formal institution was the European Coal and Steel Community (ECSC) of 1951. Following negotiation of the Treaty of Rome in 1956, it was supplemented by the European Economic Community (EEC) and the European Atomic Energy Community (EURATOM). These became collectively referred to as the European Communities, or European Community (EC). In 1992, the three institutions were integrated and renamed the European Union.

Voltaire on God, "If NATO did not exist, it would be necessary to invent it"; and the European Union's embarking on a new round of institutional creativity, both intensifying cooperation among its members and within its bodies and looking toward countries that had recently emerged from the wreckage of the Soviet Empire.

In NATO's case, it was already becoming clear that retaining the alliance and its apparatus was necessary to achieve important post–cold war purposes—ensuring that the United States would remain engaged strategically on the European continent; preserving the best of the alliance's past, including its integrated military command structure; reaching out to the newly sovereign states of Central Europe; and helping to shape Russia's future, potentially the most consequential, long-term imponderable on the continent. To fulfill its various purposes, during the 1990s, NATO embarked on a series of interlocking efforts, each designed to provide some aspect of an overall concept of security, devoted, at heart, to pursuit of the historically unprecedented chance of creating—in the words of President George H.W. Bush—a Europe "whole and free." Thus in a series of eight initiatives, NATO began taking in new members and kept the door open to others; invented the Partnership for Peace and created the Euro-Atlantic Partnership Council; signed a Founding Act with Russia and a Charter with Ukraine; revamped its command arrangements; and, at the same time, saw wisdom in developing a new relationship with the key manifestation of the old "European pillar"—the Western European Union (WEU).[2]

For its part, the European Union reached another point in its development when, periodically, it seems necessary that it move forward lest it risk falling backward—a point at which earlier efforts have been sufficiently digested to permit a reaching out for something more. Thus at Maastricht in February 1992, the EU began to craft its own post–cold war destiny and, as part of that, to renew discussion about the possibilities of European integration, including the cre-

---

[2]See, for instance, Robert E. Hunter, "Maximizing NATO," *Foreign Affairs*, Vol. 78, No. 3, May/June 1999, pp. 190–203.

ation of capacities to conduct foreign policy and, at some point, include within it a defense dimension unique to the EU.[3]

Inevitably, the parallel processes in NATO and the EU began to have
a profound impact on one another, given that they both reach the
heart of some fundamental questions, including the nature of security in 21st-century Europe; the long-term relationships among
European and transatlantic politics, economics, society, and military
affairs; the role to be played by the United States in European security—both writ large (the corpus of relations) and small (military engagement); and the precise purposes to be developed in the new era
for the two great institutions, entailing both the respective bounds
that separate them and the processes and practices that can and do
link them together.

Looking back over institutional change in NATO during the past
decade, it is in this realm—the relationship between NATO and the
European Union, represented in the defense area by the WEU and
later by the EU through what NATO has called the European Security
and Defense Identity (ESDI) and the EU has called the European
Security and Defense Policy (ESDP)[4]—that there has often seemed to

---

[3]See *Treaty on European Union*, Maastricht, February 7, 1992, especially "Title 1:
Common Provisions, Article B":

> The Union shall set itself the following objectives: . . . —to assert its identity
> on the international scene, in particular through the implementation of a
> common foreign and security policy including the eventual framing of a
> common defence policy, which might in time lead to a common defence,

which is also contained in Article J.4.

[4]"European Security and Defense Identity," "European Security and Defence Policy,"
and "Common European Security and Defence Policy (CESDP)" are terms of art.
NATO, which still proceeds with the preference for creating a European pillar within
itself, potentially drawing upon military capabilities "separable but not separate" from
the alliance, continues to use the term ESDI, which was first introduced in the
Maastricht Treaty (*Treaty on European Union*, op. cit.) of February 7, 1992. The EU, by
contrast, beginning with the Cologne European Council in June 1999, and formally at
the December 1999 Helsinki European Council, shifted to using the term ESDP, to
emphasize that this was a "policy" of the EU, and not just an "identity" derived from
NATO. Adding the "C"—for common—does not change the sense of ESDP and thus
has no great political significance; but it does bring "CESDP" into parallel with the
overarching Common Foreign and Security Policy (CFSP). It has also been argued that
CESDP is an acronym easier to handle in some EU languages than ESDP. At NATO
sometimes "identity" is used to denote NATO's part of the relationship and "policy" to

be the least amount of clarity in transatlantic debate. In each of NATO's other key initiatives, listed above—or even in the allies' dealing with the vexing issues presented by the Balkans and, more particularly, the Former Yugoslavia—there has been greater common understanding between the United States and its European partners, at least on the questions at issue; and the road to resolution, while not always smooth, especially regarding Bosnia and Kosovo, has at least been relatively straightforward.

Not so in developing the European defense pillar and its relationship to NATO—including the relationship between the European participants in this "pillar" and the United States.[5] For the better part of a decade, each new development in the creation of ESDP and in NATO's response to it has been attended by a high degree of misunderstanding, at times even mistrust, often amounting to a proper *dialogue des sourds*—a dialogue of the deaf.[6] And in few if any other

---

denote the EU's part. The terms will be used here in the sense that seems most appropriate to the text.

A senior official of NATO, who asked to remain anonymous, provides further discussion of the two terms:

> As to ESDP and ESDI, it is worth recalling that ESDP is a term of art for which the EU has exclusive proprietary rights, and the E stands for European in the sense of EU (which does not exclude, but also does not guarantee, that the EU might allow other European countries to participate in shaping it). ESDI, on the other hand, is a term which at least in part has also been shaped by NATO. The new NATO Strategic Concept of 1991, which predates the Maastricht Summit, speaks of the "creation of a European identity in security and defence" in a paragraph (22) which addresses the roles of "other European institutions such as the EC, WEU and OSCE." In 1996, we all agreed to build ESDI within the Alliance. The E in ESDI therefore has a broader connotation than in ESDP and definitely includes all European members of NATO, which unfortunately is not so clear (and in the view of some clearly not so) for ESDP (August 2001).

[5]This perception is especially striking because ten of the EU countries engaged in ESDP (eleven if Denmark, with its special status, is included) are also members of NATO. Ironically, this dual membership has not played a critical role in reducing difficulty and misunderstanding between NATO and the EU over the European pillar of the alliance; this misunderstanding clearly stems in part from the weight and influence of the United States within NATO, along with France's incomplete engagement in its integrated command structure; it may also stem in part from the habits and practices of institutions, the pull of bureaucracy, and the different cultures represented in the national delegations of the two institutions.

[6]Thus on December 5, 1998, the day after the Anglo-French summit at St. Mâlo, which was a critical turning point in the development of the European defense pillar, I

places has the lack of an intensive, open, and informed dialogue on these issues been more potentially damaging to allied comity than in the U.S. Congress. There, skepticism about ESDI-ESDP has been almost constant since about the time of the Franco-British St. Mâlo declaration (December 1998), if not before. Notably, widespread skepticism on Capitol Hill has two directly competing strands: either that ESDI will do so little that it will not make up for shortfalls in NATO capabilities—indeed, development of the European pillar could make matters worse by threatening to drain off a significant portion of what European resources are made available for defense; or that ESDI will try to do so much, at the expense of NATO's primacy, that NATO would become less effective and U.S. influence in Europe would be decisively weakened.

Part of the problem may lie in the sheer complexity of the issues and institutional developments. These have related very much to the internal workings of NATO, the WEU,[7] and the EU, and they have drawn upon decades of process and practice; they engage what all three bodies in Brussels characterize as points of "theology," of basic lore about what each institution does and what it does not do—recognizing that each is composed of sovereign states that nevertheless have learned over many years of trial and error to work effectively together, in critical and unprecedented ways. Part of the problem lies in the institutions' resistance to cooperation with one another. Part, of course, lies with the ineffable quality called "influence." This quality affects both nations and institutions and relates most profoundly to two matters: the role played by the United States in the affairs of nations on the other side of an ocean; and the classic interplay of relations among European states, now channeled at least in part through institutions designed in large part precisely for that purpose. It can also be fairly said that only a limited number of

---

attended a conference in London on transatlantic economic and security relations, organized by the Transatlantic Policy Network (TPN). Following a presentation by a senior EU official of the *St. Mâlo Communiqué* and reflecting the views of a number of U.S. members of Congress present, I asked some questions, simply for clarification of what had been agreed upon the day before. The response from several Europeans present was instantaneous and intense: Once again, the United States was interfering in a European effort to organize itself in the foreign policy and defense area! This exchange was a foretaste of what was to come in discussion and debate on the content and implications of St. Mâlo and subsequent developments.

[7]The WEU is in the process of being absorbed within the EU, in almost all functions.

people on both sides of the Atlantic have penetrated to the heart of the detailed matters at issue in the development of ESDP and its relationship to the Atlantic Alliance; yet at the same time, the essence of the basic political and security relationships between NATO and the EU is sufficiently profound to command the attention of senior leaders in all the affected countries.

The discussion that follows is not designed to be the final word on the continuing debate between NATO and the European Union—and particularly the United States and its European partners—on development of ESDP and relations between the two institutions. It is told from the point of view of one American who has been engaged in studying the issues for nearly 40 years and who negotiated NATO-WEU relations for the United States during most of the critical period in the 1990s. The discussion is thus designed to present the critical factors and issues as they evolved, in order to help elucidate them and determine which are most important and which can be viewed as extraneous. It will do so from the perspective of interests and concerns that have emerged in the United States as ESDP has developed in recent years, helping to clarify those interests and concerns for Europeans and to assess their relevance and importance for Americans.

In the process, this discussion will also point toward means for helping both NATO and the EU—as well as the United States and its European partners—to find means of creating long-term relationships regarding ESDP that can reduce inevitable frictions, as deep questions like relative political influence are pondered; and that can benefit all parties as they pursue, together, the critical common cause of promoting European security for the 21st century.

Chapter Two

INTRODUCTION

From the early days of the European Movement, launched at The Hague in 1948 under the chairmanship of Winston Churchill, the countries that later formed the European Union have had the ambition of one day creating their own foreign policy and their own defense and military institutions. This was part of trying to ensure that the tragedies of World Wars I and II would not be repeated. Thus, following the first step toward West European integration—the Schuman Plan, which became the European Coal and Steel Community in 1951—it seemed natural to try creating a European Defense Community (EDC);[1] also, as the cold war deepened, there was a requirement to find a way to rearm Western Germany and bring it into the Western alliance. The treaty that resulted, signed by six West European countries (France, Germany, Italy, and the three Benelux states) was defeated by the French parliament in 1954, mostly because it provided for too much devolution of sovereignty too soon.[2] In its place, the Western Union organization of 1948 was updated and transformed into the Western European Union—the six EDC countries and the United Kingdom—and it became the vehicle for Germany's rearmament and its parallel entry into NATO, the

---

[1]For text see *Traité Instituant la Communauté Européenne de Défense et Documents Annexes,* nouvelle édition, Paris: La Documentation Française, August 1, 1952.

[2]See Daniel Lerner and Raymond Aron, eds., *France Defeats EDC,* New York: F. A. Praeger, 1957. For a discussion of the early period of the WEU and of NATO's development, see Robert Hunter, *Security in Europe,* Bloomington: Indiana University Press, Second Edition, 1972.

paramount Western alliance, dependent on U.S. commitment, leadership, and military power.[3]

This early effort to create a European military organization thus introduced twin themes that have been present in debate and developments ever since: on the one hand, the desire of European states to move integration forward, including a defense element (and, concomitantly, arrangements for making possible a "European" foreign policy); and, on the other hand, a recognition that, for many purposes, U.S. strategic commitment, military power, and the preeminence of a U.S.-led alliance have been indispensable. Usually, these twin themes have been more-or-less compatible; but at times—like the present—they have also been a source of tension among allies.

For its part, the United States has long supported European integration, for a variety of reasons, including its own historical sense that this would reduce the risk of future conflict among states belonging to a European community, with the need for the United States thus, once again, to "sort out" European problems. Furthermore, from early-on the United States saw value in arrangements that would increase incentives for Europeans to assume a greater share of the common defense burdens that developed from the late 1940s onward. The product of these and other motives led to U.S. support for a so-called European pillar within the broader Atlantic Alliance.[4] In practice, however, during the cold war the United States imposed one major qualification: It was loath to see the European pillar develop in ways that could be fundamentally at odds with U.S. strategic objectives or overall U.S. leadership within the alliance. Within that general qualification, a minor theme was that European states might develop some limited foreign policy initiatives at variance with U.S. goals and objectives—perhaps even as an exercise in being different from America for the sake of being different, to promote European

---

[3]Spain and Portugal joined the WEU in 1990; Greece joined in 1991. Denmark, although a NATO ally that also belongs to the European Union, has chosen to remain only a WEU "observer."

[4]See François de Rose, Ambassadeur de France, "A Future Perspective for the Alliance," *NATO Review*, Vol. 43, No. 4, July 1995, pp. 9–14. Also see President John F. Kennedy, Address at Independence Hall ("Atlantic Partnership"), Philadelphia, July 4, 1962.

cohesion and integrity through opposition to Washington's lead.[5] A more important theme was what the United States believed to be the overriding strategic imperative: that Washington should have charge of the central direction of the cold war—and especially the nuclear confrontation with the Soviet Union. A European pillar could have its uses, but it must not interfere with NATO's role or the United States' lead and influence.

The end of the cold war brought a new round of discussion and decisions among the European Union countries regarding foreign policy and defense institutional arrangements, as well as a significant change in the U.S. perspective. Regarding the latter, the United States was obviously no longer concerned that security arrangements among European states could interfere with management of strategic relations with the (newly defunct) Soviet Union; indeed, the United States has come to see that the European pillar of the alliance has some particular benefits. These have included the long-term value of European integration for the recurring theme of more-equitable burden sharing. In addition, European efforts to organize for defense can be an added incentive for West European states to continue taking defense seriously, thus undertaking military efforts—and sustaining military budgets—for EU institutional reasons and, in the process, also benefiting NATO and its capabilities.

Regarding the European Union, the 1990s saw significant advances in the direction of further European integration—"deepening," in the EU's shorthand—at the same time as it was beginning to involve itself in the fate of countries in Central Europe, including the idea of eventually bringing virtually all of them fully into the union ("widening"). As progress was made in the economic and political elements of integration—leading, most dramatically, to the January 1999 introduction of a common currency, the Euro, among 11 of the 15 member states—it was natural that the union turned again toward developing a Common Foreign and Security Policy (CFSP) and, as

---

[5]Thus, as the European Community (EC) began trying to develop a fledgling foreign policy, there were constant struggles over the extent to which the United States could be given access to deliberations while they were still in process. One approach was the "Gymnich Formula," whereby a troika of leaders—immediately past, present, and immediately future presidencies of the EC—could brief the Americans on what the EC states were discussing within their "European Political Cooperation" (EPC).

part of it, a European Security and Defense Identity (ESDI)—now called by the EU the European Security and Defense Policy (ESDP). These initiatives were set forth as goals and as practical steps in the EU treaties of Maastricht (1992) and Amsterdam (1997).[6] In the realm of defense, efforts focused on being able to undertake a range of military missions, the so-called Petersberg Tasks, so named for a WEU council of ministers' meeting in June 1992.[7] These potential missions, as later incorporated in the Amsterdam Treaty, would "include humanitarian and rescue tasks, peacekeeping tasks and tasks of combat forces in crisis management, including peace-making."[8] Notably, NATO allies rapidly pledged support for the new ESDI.[9]

---

[6] *Title V: Provisions on a Common Foreign and Security Policy.* Maastricht (*The Single European Act of 1992*) laid out the framework for CFSP and set as a goal "the eventual framing of a common defence policy, which might in time lead to a common defence" (Article J.4.1). The WEU was asked "to elaborate and implement decisions and actions of the Union which have defence implications" (Article J.4.2). However, member state obligations under the North Atlantic Treaty were respected, and EU policy was to be "compatible with the common security and defence policy established within that [North Atlantic Treaty] framework" (Article J.4.4). At the same time, the Maastricht Treaty's "Final Act" included a declaration by the then nine members of the WEU that the "Member States of WEU welcome the development of the European security and defence identity" (ibid.). Thus the term ESDI was launched.

The Amsterdam Treaty went beyond Maastricht, referring to the "progressive framing of a common defence policy . . . which might lead to a common defence, should the European Council so decide" (paragraph 17.1, Title V of the *Consolidated Version of the Treaty on European Union*). Amsterdam provided for "the possibility of the integration of the WEU into the Union, should the European Council so decide" (ibid.). Also, "The progressive framing of a common defence policy will be supported, as Member States consider appropriate, by cooperation between them in the field of armaments" (ibid.). In addition, when the EU used the WEU "to elaborate and implement decisions of the Union," all member states would be "entitled to participate fully in the tasks in question" (ibid., paragraph 17.3). That meant inclusion of EU members that are not also members of NATO.

[7] See Western European Union Council of Ministers, *Petersberg Declaration*, Bonn, June 19, 1992, paragraph II.4.

[8] *Consolidated Version of the Treaty on European Union*, Title V, Article 17.2. The very limited nature of these Petersberg tasks is sometimes overlooked, by both some European proponents and some U.S. critics of ESDP.

[9] See NATO, Ministerial Meeting of the North Atlantic Council, *Final Communiqué*, M-NAC-2(93)70, Brussels, December 2, 1993, paragraph 2:

> Foreign Ministers . . . reaffirmed their full support for the emerging European Security and Defence Identity and for the further development of close cooperation between NATO and WEU on the basis of transparency and complementarity. They believe that this will contribute to strengthening

the European pillar and, by doing so, the Alliance itself, and result in a
strengthened and more equal transatlantic partnership.

Chapter Three

THE GRAND BARGAIN OF BERLIN AND BRUSSELS

Thus the NATO allies and the members of the Western European Union—acting, in effect, as the executive agent for ESDI—began negotiating to determine what, in practice, it could mean and what ESDI's relationship should properly be with NATO. These negotiations led to a grand bargain, prompted mainly by economic necessity, but also by a widely shared sense that NATO and WEU should not find themselves at loggerheads over roles and missions for post–cold war security in Europe. On the one hand, the WEU states wanted a capacity to take military actions if and when NATO were not inclined to act—by implication, that meant abstention by the United States. On the other hand, the United States and some other allies were concerned that few if any European states would provide the resources needed for a full-fledged WEU, in addition to NATO—there were simply not enough resources to create two sets of military forces. There were also concerns that promoting a WEU that was truly independent of NATO could weaken the latter's capacity to act.

Thus emerged the grand bargain: The NATO Alliance would help to facilitate the creation of ESDI, but not as a completely independent entity, likely to rob NATO both of resources and, potentially, of capacity to be politically and militarily effective. Instead, ESDI would be built within NATO, possibly drawing upon military capabilities "separable but not separate" from the alliance. This implied that a portion of the NATO structure would be made available for use by the WEU—ready to be "borrowed," as it were—and thereby becoming a European pillar that was truly of, rather than separate from, the Atlantic Alliance.

Major impetus for concluding this grand bargain, which was negotiated at NATO's Berlin and Brussels foreign and defense ministerial
meetings in June 1996, came from twin initiatives.[1] The first was
taken by America's first post–cold war administrations, under Presi-
dents George H.W. Bush and Bill Clinton: The former blessed the
"expression of a common European foreign and security policy and
defense role";[2] the latter elaborated the NATO part of the potential
grand bargain at the Brussels summit meeting of January 1994, including the idea that NATO stood "ready to make collective assets of
the Alliance available . . . for WEU operations."[3] This was to be done
on the basis of a critical concept alluded to above: "separable but not
separate military capabilities that could be employed by NATO or the
WEU."[4] In response, a second initiative came from the French gov-

---

[1]For details of the "grand bargain," see Ministerial Meeting of the North Atlantic
Council, *Final Communiqué*, Berlin, NATO Press Communiqué M-NAC-1(96)63, June
3, 1996; and Meeting of the North Atlantic Council in Defence Ministers' Session, *Final
Communiqué*, Brussels, NATO Press Communiqué M-NAC(DM)-2(96)89, June 13,
1996.

[2]See Heads of State and Government Participating in the Meeting of the North Atlantic
Council, *Rome Declaration on Peace and Cooperation*, Rome, Press Communiqué S-
1(91)86, November 8, 1991, paragraphs 6–8. Nevertheless, not long before U.S.
administrations changed, Washington presented the allies with a list of "don'ts" regarding the development of a European defense capability that rankled many Europeans for some time, especially because the United States was holding back on com-
mitting forces to help bring peace to Yugoslavia. See Fraser Cameron, *Europe,
Yugoslavia and the Blame Game*, American Foreign Service Association, 2000
(www.afsa.org/fsi/feb00/cameron.html):

> When the fighting started, the Bush administration publicly supported E.U.
> efforts to achieve a negotiated solution but categorically ruled out commit-
> ting U.S. troops to Yugoslavia. Yet the U.S. also sent a demarche, the
> [Reginald] Bartholomew/[James] Dobbins letter, warning the E.U. not to de-
> velop an independent defense capability.

See also Martin Walker, "The European Union and the European Security and Defense
Initiative," *NATO & Europe in the 21st Century*, Woodrow Wilson International Center
for Scholars, 2000 (www.wwics.si.edu/ees/special/2000/apr00.htm): "The U.S. Bush
Administration had made it clear (in the celebrated Bartholomew letter) that such
one-sided European experiments [as ESDI] could put NATO at risk."

[3]See Ministerial Meeting of the North Atlantic Council/North Atlantic Cooperation
Council, *Declaration of the Heads of State and Government*, NATO Headquarters,
Brussels, Press Communiqué M-1(94)3, January 10–11, 1994, particularly paragraphs
3–6.

[4]Ibid., paragraph 9. Also see Warren Christopher, "Towards a NATO Summit," *NATO
Review*, Vol. 431, No. 4, August 1993, pp. 3–6 (www.nato.int/docu/review/1993/9304-

ernment of President Jacques Chirac on December 5, 1995, coupling support for creating an effective relationship between NATO and the WEU with the setting of conditions whereby France would be prepared to rejoin NATO's integrated military command, from which it had departed in 1966.[5]

The grand bargain sealed at Berlin and Brussels in June 1996 had several key elements, of which the following were most important:[6]

- There could be "WEU-led" operations, including "planning and exercising of command elements and forces."

- NATO would identify "types of separable but not separate capabilities, assets and support assets . . . HQs [Headquarters], HQ elements and command structures . . . which could be made available, subject to decision by the [North Atlantic Council]" and subsequent "monitoring of the use" of these forces by NATO. This continuing role of NATO in the use of its "assets" was later broadened to provide for their "return or recall," if they proved to be needed by the alliance—e.g., in the event of a competing crisis or conflict.[7]

1.htm): "we must act on the premise that although the military capabilities of the two institutions [NATO and WEU] are separable, they must not be seen as separate."

[5]See M. Hervé de Charette, *Intervention du Ministre des Affaires Etrangeres,* Session Ministerielle du Conseil de l'Atlantique Nord, Bruxelles, December 5, 1995. France rejoined the NATO Military Committee and also took other steps including the start of "un processus de nature a ameliorer nos relations de travail avec le quartier général allié en Europe (SHAPE)." This, de Charette declared, was in response to the adaptation of the structures of the alliance, agreed at the Brussels summit, especially in regard to the provision of "collective assets": "les moyens de l'Alliance." Further, he cited "l'emergence d'une identité européenne visible, sur le plan militaire comme sur le plan politique, au sein de l'Alliance." If the allies would join France in working for adapting the alliance, "nous pourrons envisager, dans des étapes ulterieures des rapprochements avec d'autres organes de l'Alliance atlantique."

[6]See, in particular, Ministerial Meeting of the North Atlantic Council, June 3, 1996, paragraph 7, op. cit.

[7]See Meeting of the North Atlantic Council in Defence Ministers' Session, *Final Communiqué,* NATO Press Release M-NAC-D-1(97)71, June 12, 1997, paragraph 7. Also see Ministerial Meeting of the North Atlantic Council, *Final Communiqué,* Brussels, Press Release M-NAC-D-1(98)71, June 11, 1998, paragraph 14:

> further steps have been taken, in close cooperation with the WEU, on: . . . the elaboration of arrangements for the release, monitoring and return or recall of NATO assets and capabilities in the context of a WEU-led operation with NATO support.

- Multinational European command arrangements within NATO would be worked out for WEU-led operations (including planning and exercising)—i.e., "double hatting" of NATO personnel, who could be detached for use by the WEU.[8] At the same time, NATO agreed that its Deputy Supreme Allied Commander Europe (DSACEUR) could be used by the WEU as its own strategic commander in the event of a WEU military operation.

- ESDI could take advantage of NATO's newly developed concept of the Combined Joint Task Force (CJTF) headquarters, an instrument that could be made available for use by the WEU as well as by NATO. Indeed, CJTF could provide a mechanism for enabling the WEU to be effective without having to duplicate military command arrangements; it would get these "ready made" from NATO.

- All European members of NATO would be able to take part in WEU-led operations, including European command arrangements if they chose to do so (this was in particular a reference to Turkey).[9]

There was also agreement that the alliance—i.e., NATO—would remain the "essential forum" for security consultations and pursuit of "common security objectives"; that the allies were ready "to pursue common security objectives through the [NATO] Alliance, wherever possible;" and that there would be "full transparency between NATO

Also see *Annual Report of the WEU Council to the WEU Assembly*, July 1 to December 31, 1998, Section I: "Progress was made towards a 'framework' setting out principles and modalities for the transfer, monitoring and return or recall of NATO assets and capabilities for WEU-led operations."

[8]For example, a

WEU-NATO Crisis Management Workshop held on 10 September 1998 reviewed procedures for consultations in the event of a WEU-led operation using NATO assets and capabilities, and opened up new prospects for achieving fully harmonised, practicable arrangements in this field (*Annual Report of the WEU Council to the WEU Assembly*, July 1 to December 31, 1998, op. cit.).

[9]The defence ministers' communiqué further put the point as follows: "the building, with the participation of all Allies, of the ESDI within the Alliance" (Meeting of the North Atlantic Council in Defence Ministers' Session, June 13, 1996, op. cit., paragraph 11).

and the WEU in crisis management."[10] These were not trivial points, recognizing implicitly NATO's primacy, and especially the critical role played by the United States in post–cold war European security. Part of the bargain, worked out over time, was also that NATO would have first call on forces designated for other European multinational forces—e.g., the EUROCORPS, EUROFOR, and EUROMARFOR.[11]

---

[10]See Ministerial Meeting of the North Atlantic Council, June 3, 1996, op. cit., paragraph 7:

> the Alliance as the essential forum for consultation among its members and the venue for agreement on policies bearing on the security and defence commitments of Allies under the Washington Treaty; . . . readiness to pursue common security objectives through the Alliance, wherever possible; full transparency between NATO and WEU in crisis management, including as necessary through joint consultations on how to address contingencies.

This language drew upon the Heads of State and Government Participating in the Meeting of the North Atlantic Council, November 8, 1991 (*Rome Declaration* of November 1991), op. cit., paragraph 6. Arrangements were also to be made for NATO to do military planning and exercises for "illustrative WEU missions identified by the WEU." This provision recognized that (1) WEU could not very well act during a crisis if it had not at least thought through what contingencies might arise; (2) it did not have the resources to do such planning on its own; but (3) it would be unrealistic for NATO to try planning for every possible WEU operation: Hence NATO would consider "illustrative" operations—i.e., a limited range of possible scenarios.

[11]See Ministerial Meeting of the North Atlantic Council, NATO Headquarters, Brussels, *Press Communiqué* M-NAC-2(92)106, December 17, 1992, paragraph 12; Ministerial Meeting of the North Atlantic Council, NATO Headquarters, Brussels, *Press Communiqué* M-NAC-2(95)118, December 5, 1995, paragraph 9:

> We welcome the prospect of all of these multinational capabilities becoming available to NATO as well as to the WEU, in keeping with the existing NATO commitments of participating nations, and we look forward to the early definition of the relationship of EUROFOR and EUROMARFOR to NATO.

See also Meeting of the North Atlantic Council in Defence Ministers' Session, Brussels, Press Communiqué M-NAC(DM)-3(96)172, December 18, 1996, paragraph 22; and CRS, *German-American Relations in the New Europe*, Issue Brief 81018, December 5, 1996:

> On November 30, 1992, France and Germany announced that the Eurocorps could be placed under NATO command, in the case of an attack on the alliance or of a decision by NATO governments to dispatch a peacekeeper force outside alliance territory. On January 21, 1993, an official agreement was signed on the terms of cooperation between NATO and the Eurocorps, thus ending fears that the Eurocorps would undermine NATO.

Members of the EUROCORPS are Belgium, France, Germany, Luxembourg, and Spain. "The Eurofor (rapid deployment force) and Euromarfor (maritime force) include

Critically important was an additional point pinned down at the June 1996 NATO defense ministers' meeting in Brussels after difficult negotiations between France and the United States: There should be a "single, multinational command structure, *respecting the principle of unity of command* [emphasis added]."[12] These critical seven words (in italics) represented agreement that, whatever NATO "assets" were to be made available to the WEU, it should be done in a way that NATO's capacity to act would not be impaired, nor would there be "two NATOs"—one for implementing requirements under Article 5 of the Washington Treaty of 1949 ("the North Atlantic Treaty") and one for so-called non-Article 5 operations, such as peacekeeping or peacemaking. In effect, if the new ESDI were "separated" from NATO, the capacity of the latter to act effectively would not—at least in theory—be impaired in any material way.[13]

In short, the Berlin and Brussels agreements of June 1996 created the possibility that the WEU, for the first time, might become a militarily effective organization, able to respond to at least some of the limited range of agreed Petersberg Tasks, while at the same time the agreements ratified the essential links across the Atlantic and, it can be argued, the implicit concept of "NATO first"—although this concept was never formally agreed to. Little noted at the time was a critical implication behind the key provision for "separable but not separate [NATO] capabilities, assets, and support assets" to be made available for the WEU's use. Of course, NATO, as an institution, "owns" very little in terms of military capabilities and assets but must rely upon what individual allies are prepared to commit for use, on request, by

---

forces from France, Italy, Portugal and Spain" (*NATO Handbook*, Chapter 15, "The Wider Institutional Framework for Security," May 8, 2001).

[12]This point was made in the context of NATO's *Long-Term Study*, which was on the alliance's command structure, but it was included to clarify the Berlin agreement on ESDI (see Ministerial Meeting of the North Atlantic Council, June 3, 1996, op. cit., paragraph 8). The seven words, critical to success of the negotiations, were suggested by the Chairman of the NATO Military Committee, German General Klaus Naumann, in conversation with the author, who, along with his German colleague on the North Atlantic Council, introduced them into the negotiations.

[13]See also the Meeting of the North Atlantic Council in Defence Ministers' Session, June 13, 1996, op. cit., regarding "the concept of one system capable of performing multiple functions."

the alliance's military commands.[14] Thus, as European allies con-templated what "capabilities and assets" they lacked and would have to seek from NATO, they found that, in some critical areas—including large transport aircraft, sophisticated intelligence, and satellite-based communications—the primary storehouse of capacity be-longed, in fact, to the United States. As a result, as part of the grand bargain of 1996, the United States agreed that some of its own forces—although not combat personnel, as such—could be made available to the WEU and serve under its command. This could even include circumstances where the United States chose not to become fully engaged, as opposed to circumstances in which the United States *did* take part and in which NATO would therefore be fully in charge and would act according to its practices and procedures.[15]

---

[14]NATO's "ownership" of military goods is largely limited to headquarters; command, control, and communications facilities; to some logistics (like the NATO Pipeline System); and to 17 Airborne Warning and Control surveillance aircraft.

[15]It is not clear that more than a few members of the U.S. Congress have understood the full import of this agreement regarding the potential role of U.S. forces—including noncombat military personnel who could still be exposed to hostile fire—under the command of the Western European Union.

Chapter Four

BEYOND BERLIN: DEVIL IN THE DETAILS (I)

The agreement reached at NATO's Berlin and Brussels ministerial meetings in June 1996 could have been the end of the basic debate within the alliance about the development of the European defense pillar—an elegant arrangement between two institutions, respecting the interests and ambitions of each. But this was not to be, in part because of the need to work out the practical details of the relationship between NATO and the WEU.

Furthermore, from the U.S. point of view (acting informally as lead custodian of the NATO position), some points of the grand bargain did raise questions. For example, the Brussels and Washington Treaties both contain commitments for allies to come to one another's aid in the event of external aggression, according to particular definitions; indeed, the Brussels Treaty does more to commit its member states to take military action than does the Washington Treaty—at least in theory, although not in practice, since the WEU does not have either a serious military structure or the political and strategic engagement of the United States.[1] The United States was concerned, however, that a European country that was not a member of NATO might join the WEU, because of either its membership in the European Union or the invitation extended to other states by

---

[1]See the *Modified Brussels Treaty,* October 23, 1994: Each high contracting party will "afford the Party so attacked all the military and other aid and assistance in [its] power" (Article V). Compare this with the North Atlantic Treaty: Each ally will join in taking "such action as it deems necessary, including the use of armed force" (Article 5).

the Maastricht EU summit of December 1991.[2] If such a country were subjected to external aggression, the other WEU states would have to come to its aid with "all the military and other aid and assistance in their power;" and, in practice, that would mean exposing NATO to risks, as well. For Washington, this raised the possibility that it could, in practice, become committed to taking military action without having had a say in how a crisis got to that point: Countries could, in effect, enter NATO through the "back door." Thus the United States adopted a formal position that any WEU member would also have to be a NATO member—a position that could have real substance, given that the European Union, like NATO, was embarking on a process of enlarging to include countries in Central Europe. However, although the United States did come to support an "open door" for membership in the alliance, it was quick to point out that it was not implying that it would support NATO membership for any country that happened to find its way into the EU and thus chose to join the WEU; rather, Washington was, in effect, asking for a veto on any country that takes this path, unless, by its own volition, NATO also grants admittance.[3]

In theory, this was a serious issue for the United States and hence for the alliance. In practice, however, it has had far less strength, since there has not appeared to be much risk that any WEU member would be the victim of external aggression. Furthermore, if that were to

---

[2] See *Maastricht Declarations*, December 10, 1991, II. Declaration:

> States which are members of the European Union are invited to accede to WEU on conditions to be agreed in accordance with Article XI of the modified Brussels Treaty, or to become observers if they so wish.

[3] See Robert E. Hunter, *E.S.D.I. and the Future of Transatlantic Relations*, Jean Monnet CFSP Working Paper No. 7, Brussels, Spring 1998:

> [T]here are U.S. concerns well known, that members of WEU should also be members of NATO. . . . And for the United States, there is the desire not to see backdoor membership to NATO, but rather members through the front door. This implies a continued American willingness to support the open door to NATO membership so that there can be a correspondence of countries that eventually join WEU and the Atlantic Alliance itself.

Also see Wim van Eeekelen, General Rapporteur, *EU, WEU, and NATO: Towards a European Security and Defence Identity*, NATO Parliamentary Assembly, Sub-committee on Defence and Security Co-operation between Europe and North America, October 6, 1999, paragraph 23 (www.bits.de/CESD-PA/Parlrep-van-Eekelen-April-99-Draft-as110dscdc-e.html).

happen, it would probably be under circumstances where NATO (including the United States) would be prepared to defend the nation so attacked, whether or not there were formal treaty commitments. Additionally, none of the four former "neutral and non-aligned" countries that now belong to the EU but not to NATO chose to avail itself of the right to join the WEU as full members, but rather (at Rome in December 1992) became "observers"—in some cases at least in part to avoid challenging the declared U.S. position.[4] Thus Washington chose not to press the point; but for the future, there remains an issue whether new members of the EU and hence participants in ESDP will be accorded the protections of Article V of the Brussels Treaty.[5]

---

[4]The "Final Act" of the Maastricht Treaty (*Treaty on European Union,* February 7, 1992, op. cit.) provided that

> members of the European Union are invited to accede to WEU on condi-
> tions to be agreed in accordance with Article XI of the modified Brussels
> Treaty, or to become observers if they so wish. Simultaneously, other
> European Member States of NATO are invited to become associate members
> of WEU in a way which will give them the possibility of participating fully in
> the activities of WEU. The Member States of WEU assume that treaties and
> agreements corresponding with above proposals will be concluded before
> 31 December 1992.

Thus the four former "neutral and non-aligned" countries presumably lost their right to affect WEU policy in the style of full members. However, see footnote 6, below.

[5]See, for instance, Van Eeekelen, October 6, 1999, op. cit.,

> Dropping Article V [of the Brussels Treaty for new WEU/ESDP members]
> would be a step back in terms of solidarity. Maintaining it should not be dif-
> ficult, as nobody foresees this cause being implemented outside the collec-
> tive defence provided by NATO. This point also gives the answer to US
> concerns about "back-door" guarantees if the EU and WEU admit new
> members who do not wish—or are unable—to join NATO as well. Today the
> question does not seem urgent, but could become topical when EU
> enlargement gathers momentum. It would be difficult to exclude new
> members of the European security framework simply because NATO is not
> ready to take them in.

See also Cologne European Council, *Presidency Conclusions,* June 3–4, 1999, "Annex III, European Council Declaration on Strengthening the Common European Policy on Security and Defence," paragraph 2:

> The commitments under Article 5 of the Washington Treaty and Article V of
> the Brussels Treaty will in any event be preserved for the Member States
> party to these Treaties. The policy of the Union shall not prejudice the spe-
> cific character of the security and defence policy of certain Member States.

The U.S. government was also concerned about one particular aspect of the EU's development of its Common Foreign and Security Policy, which entailed the capacity for the EU to direct the WEU's actions. The Amsterdam Treaty provided that all EU members would be able to act on an "equal footing," which included making decisions about what the WEU should do to undertake any of the Petersberg Tasks.[6] That provision clearly indicated that the EU's process of "taking" decisions about the WEU would include states that were not also members of NATO (at the time Finland, Sweden, Austria, and Ireland) with the last not then even a member of NATO's Partnership for Peace (PFP).[7] Thus, such countries would be in a position potentially of shaping NATO policy—and certainly of gaining access to NATO proprietary information—without also sharing in the responsibilities and practices, explicit and implicit, of NATO membership. In time, the WEU might also include, as full members, Central European

---

Also see "German Proposal on ESDI Unveiled," *NATO News and Analysis,* March 16, 1999:

> The commitments under Article 5 of the Washington Treaty and Article V of the Brussels Treaty will be preserved although there will be a need to review the institutional basis for the latter, in the understanding that whatever happens to the modified Brussels Treaty Article V, *the collective security guarantee will continue to apply only to those who are NATO allies* [emphasis added].

In addition, see House of Commons Defence Committee, Written Evidence, *Memorandum by Richard G. Whitman, University of Westminster, and Karen E Smith, London School of Economics,* July 26, 2000 (www.parliament.the-stationery-office. co.uk/pa/cm199900/cmselect/cmdfence/295/295we01.htm):

> [I]mporting Article V into the EU Treaty will be extremely difficult, given the implications this poses for the neutral states in particular, as well as for the future development of the EU.

[6] See *The Single European Act of 1992* (Maastricht Treaty), February 7, 1992, op. cit., Title V, Article J.4. Also see *Consolidated Version of the Treaty on European Union,* op. cit., Title V, paragraph 17.3:

> When the Union avails itself of the WEU to elaborate and implement decisions of the Union on the [Petersberg] tasks . . . all Member States of the Union shall be entitled to participate fully in the tasks in question. [This would include participating] fully and on an equal footing in decision-taking in the WEU.

[7] Ireland did join PFP on November 1, 1999, thus agreeing to take part in a formal relationship with a military alliance for the first time in its history as an independent state.

states that joined the European Union but not also NATO—an issue that has not arisen so far but that could do so in the future. However, while potentially serious, this problem had no practical solution without provoking a clash between NATO and the European Union, at a time when the issue remained moot: So long as the WEU was quiescent, there was no need to push this matter to the level of major debate and disagreement.

Concerns about the grand bargain also appeared on the European side, and in particular in France. It remained unconvinced that the agreed arrangements, along with the broader framework of under-standings about its overall relationship to NATO, would meet its na-tional requirements. Most visibly, within a few months after the Berlin-Brussels decisions, France and the United States entered into a major dispute over command arrangements within NATO, a dispute central to the question whether France would rejoin the NATO integrated military command structure or would stop at the halfway house of rejoining NATO's Military Committee, which it did in December 1995.[8] The proximate cause of the dispute was the disposition of one of Allied Command Europe's two major subordinate military commands—Allied Forces Southern Europe (AFSOUTH), headquartered in Naples. Noting that the United States provided commanding officers for NATO's two principal commands, Allied Command Europe (Casteau/Mons) and Allied Command Atlantic (Norfolk), France insisted that subordinate commands in Europe be headed by Europeans; indeed, this had long since been the case for Allied Forces Central Europe (Brunssum, Netherlands); and, France argued, this arrangement should logically and politically also apply to AFSOUTH.[9]

---

[8]See, for instance, Voice of America, December 5, 1995, www.hri.org/news/agencies/voa/95-12-05_1.voa.html; and Ministerial Meeting of the North Atlantic Council held at NATO Headquarters, *Final Communiqué,* Brussels, December 5, 1995, Press Communiqué M-NAC-2(95)118, paragraph 2. This was part of Chirac's decision to move in the direction of full membership of the integrated command structure. Henceforth, as well, France again took part in meetings of NATO defense ministers. For this purpose, supplementing the Defense Planning Committee (DPC), which had been the "NATO Ministers minus France" forum since the mid-1960s, the allies created a parallel forum, named according to the author's suggestion, "the North Atlantic Council in Defense Ministers Session."

[9]This French request came only after a more grandiose proposal had been rejected by the United States as unworkable and politically unsustainable, for both the United

By contrast, the United States insisted that it retain control of this command, because of the major role its forces play in the Mediterranean and the difficulty of explaining to the U.S. Congress that American forces serving in the Former Yugoslavia (a theater commanded by AFSOUTH) were not under U.S. command;[10] but Washington did say that, at such time (if ever) that the Europeans showed that they were pulling greater strategic weight than the United States in terms of naval combat power in the Mediterranean region, the command arrangements could be reviewed and, by implication, changed.[11]

In part because of this impasse, Paris concluded that the alliance had not been sufficiently reformed, as requested by President Chirac in

---

States and the alliance as a whole. This request was to create a sort of "super" Supreme Allied Commander, a post to be held by an American officer, while the positions both of Supreme Allied Commander Europe (SACEUR) and Supreme Allied Commander Atlantic (SACLANT) would be held by European officers. See *AFSOUTH and Command Structure Reform: How AFSOUTH Fits In,* Institute for National Strategic Studies, www.ndu.edu/inss/books/afsouth/afsaf.html:

> President Chirac recommended that NATO's top command be organized around a U.S.-designated super-SACEUR at the head of a single strategic command, with two sub-strategic commands correlating to the current MNCs except that the MNC command position in Europe would be filled by a European.

Note: The proposal made by the French government to the American government was for both Major NATO Commands (MNCs) to be headed by Europeans.

[10]See, for example, Press Briefing by Undersecretary of Defense for Policy Walter Slocombe and U.S. Permanent Representative to NATO Robert E. Hunter, Meeting of the North Atlantic Cooperation Council in Defence Ministers Session, NATO HQ, Brussels, December 17, 1996 (www.nato.int/docu/speech/1996/s961217d.htm):

> Ambassador Hunter: . . . We have said, as the United States—and on this we have the broad backing of most of the Allies—that it is essential for us in terms of American engagement here and the weight of American strategic power that in the restructuring of commands we retain the command in AFSOUTH.

[11]See ibid.:

> Ambassador Hunter: . . . in terms of meeting the desires expressed by a number of European countries, including France, for a greater role for Europeans, greater responsibility, more command slots going to Europeans, greater visibility, all of this is in strict conformance with what we would like to do, as well. And we are pleased to discuss a wide range of alternatives with regard to that. And on that basis, I suspect we'll find a way to move this to conclusion.

December 1995, to justify its full return to NATO's integrated military command structure. This dispute, largely opaque to any outside observer who lacked a thorough knowledge of NATO lore and detailed command structures, helped to spur disagreements that still continue regarding the future of the European Security and Defense Policy and its relationship to NATO. Just as the political possibilities for the Berlin-Brussels grand bargain were tied up with France's overall relationship to NATO, so the future of NATO–EU/ESDP relations cannot be disentangled from this broader question of alliance reform, with all of its political implications.

At the same time, France (with some often-quiet support from other European allies) had doubts about particular aspects of the 1996 grand bargain. For example, the North Atlantic Council would retain authority over the release of NATO assets for WEU use—thus preserving veto power for the United States (with its preeminence in ownership of national military assets that the WEU was likely to want to use); and Washington was clearly loath to approve any language that would imply that this release would be "automatic." The obvious question was thus posed: Would the United States be willing, when actually challenged, to take the final step—to implement its pledge, even to put some of its own military personnel under WEU command, outside of the NATO command structure—or would it balk at the last moment?[12] Obviously, there is no way to test this proposition in advance, and in recent years the United States has shown considerable reluctance to put its forces in harm's way without a conflict's having a direct connection to U.S. interests and values. Furthermore, despite the 1996 Berlin and Brussels agreements, France was not reconciled to the view that NATO needed to remain preeminent as a European security organization for military operations that did not fall under the Washington Treaty's Article 5 (response to external attack) as well as for those that did; and, according to the Berlin-Brussels arrangements, NATO would have this

---

[12]For some observers, this has remained an unreal debate, since, at least for the next several years, it does not appear likely that there would be any call for the WEU (EU)—through ESDP—to act militarily at any significant level of activity without the United States' willingness to take part—at least in Europe or directly affecting its own security—in which case the operation would fall under NATO. The 1999 conflict over Kosovo seemed to validate this point. Of course, as argued elsewhere, an operation in Africa could be a different story.

preeminence even though, for non-Article 5 military operations—that is, the operations most likely to be conducted in post–cold war Europe—it was likely that European forces would undertake the bulk of the fighting, at least in a ground campaign.[13]

Thus the issue of the WEU's relationship to NATO, at the heart of the development of ESDI, continued to engage an underlying political competition between France and (primarily) the United States. This was doubly true because of what was widely believed to be a basic French motive for championing ESDI: It represented a realm of activity (military) in which France could exercise a major leadership role within Europe, including vis-à-vis Germany—a country virtually guaranteed, in major part because of German Unification, to have decisive economic, and hence overall political, preeminence within the European Union; but Germany was also a country that was still limited, politically, in its ability to employ military power, as witnessed in its tentative approach to engagement in the Bosnia conflict.[14]

---

[13]In fact, during the Kosovo War of 1999, the United States undertook the vast bulk of military operations in this "non-Article 5" conflict. Of course, in part that was because the alliance elected to rely almost exclusively on air power, thus avoiding ground operations—with far higher risks of allied casualties—in which European allies would have had a much more prominent role.

[14]Of course, this is very likely to be a wasting asset for France, as Germany gains more confidence and experience in deploying combat forces, within the context either of NATO or of the EU/ESDP. But it should still be several years before France loses its political advantages in this sphere.

Chapter Five

ST. MÂLO AND BEYOND

Despite these and other continuing concerns on both sides of the Atlantic about the relationship between NATO and the WEU, ESDI was not a major topic of political discussion or controversy for more than two years after the 1996 grand bargain. But it suddenly reemerged from the bureaucratic doldrums on December 4, 1998, only a few weeks before the Euro was launched among 11 (now 12) of the 15 EU countries (known as "Euroland"), notably not including the United Kingdom. Presumably at least in part to demonstrate its engagement in a major project leading toward completion of European integration, the British government of Prime Minister Tony Blair reversed its long-standing position of remaining relatively aloof from ESDI and, indeed, of being a leading proponent of European skepticism about its prospects.[1] Blair and Chirac met at St. Mâlo and issued a brief statement that gave new life both to ESDI and to debate about it within the alliance.[2]

---

[1]St. Mâlo gave Britain, which had not joined the European Monetary Union or subscribed to the Euro, a chance to appear committed to the European "vocation"; further, it enabled London to throw in its lot with Paris, where the latter had much at stake in its twin competitions for influence with Germany (the greater) and the United States (the lesser). Provided that Britain could convince the United States that it was not straying from its basic allegiance to NATO—or straining at the "special relationship" with Washington—this was a sustainable position. Indeed, on the morrow of St. Mâlo, one of its British negotiators said to the TPN meeting in London, with its clutch of U.S. members of Congress, that Britain would never countenance any interpretation of St. Mâlo that could weaken NATO's primacy.

[2]See *Text of a Joint Statement by the British and French Governments,* Franco-British Summit, Saint-Mâlo, France, December 4, 1998.

The St. Mâlo declaration was widely examined for what it included and what it left out. Indeed, its construction permitted a wide range of interpretations, and those by British and French officials immediately began emphasizing quite different parts of the declaration. Much of it drew on prior EU agreements, although they had rarely been gathered together and highlighted politically in this way. Also, St. Mâlo's emphasis that decisions about the use of an ESDI would be made by the European Union and not by the WEU elicited comment, especially in Washington; but this position was consistent with EU decisions going back to the Maastricht summit of 1992.[3]

At first reading, the St. Mâlo declaration was simply a call for speeding up the process of implementing what had been agreed upon at the June 1997 Amsterdam EU summit on CFSP, including the "progressive framing of a common defence policy." The declaration also made the standard and obligatory bow to the Atlantic Alliance as "the foundation of the collective defence of its members." But it also appeared to break new ground. While it honored the collective defense provisions of the Washington Treaty's Article 5, it was silent on the Berlin-Brussels agreements about NATO's (implicit) primacy and the notion that there should not be "two NATOs"—one for Article 5 and one for non-Article 5 tasks. Absent also was the explicit idea of an ESDI within the NATO framework that could make use of "separable but not separate" military capabilities. In addition, although the

---

[3]See *Treaty on European Union,* op. cit., Article J.4:

2. The union requests the Western European Union (WEU), which is an integral part of the development of the Union, to elaborate and implement decisions and actions of the Union which have defence implications. The Council shall, in agreement with the institutions of the WEU, adopt the necessary practical arrangements.

3. Issues having defence implications dealt with under this Article shall not be subject to the procedures set out in Article J.3.

4. The policy of the Union in accordance with this Article shall not prejudice the specific character of the security and defence policy of certain Member States and shall respect the obligations of certain Member States under the North Atlantic Treaty and be compatible with the common security and defence policy established within that framework.

Note the ambiguity in paragraph 3, relating to the decisionmaking process (including qualified majorities) of the preceding section of the treaty.

declaration did mention in this context, as part of a list of sources for military capabilities, those "pre-designated within NATO's European pillar," it also asserted that "the Union must have the capacity for *autonomous* action" [emphasis added]. This phrase, appearing in the declaration for the first time—and not clearly defined—has continued to bedevil discussion across the Atlantic.[4]

At the same time, the St. Mâlo declaration argued that the European Union would need its own "appropriate structures and a capacity" to analyze situations, have sources of intelligence, and undertake strategic planning—clear references to areas where either NATO as a whole or the United States in particular had preeminence and where, therefore, the Europeans would be dependent on U.S. willingness to "release [U.S.] assets." But the declaration also noted both that military action would take place "when the Alliance as a whole is not engaged," and that these European capacities should be developed "without unnecessary duplication." Remarkably, debate still continues across the Atlantic about ESDP regarding the issues covered by these two phrases, as though they had not been included in the St. Mâlo declaration or repeated several times since.[5]

Perhaps most important, however, was that the St. Mâlo declaration was agreed upon between Britain and France, with little or no ad-

---

[4]In retrospect, French Defense Minister Alain Richard argued that St. Mâlo

> stressed 4 important points: all nations of the Union were invited to take part, no loss of sovereignty was envisaged, new and real capabilities had to be built, the European security and defense policy was consistent with the role and responsibility of NATO (see speech by Alain Richard, French Minister of Defense, at the Annual Defense Dinner of the London Chamber of Commerce and Industry, London, May 17, 2001, www.info-france-usa.org/news/statmnts/eurodefe.htm).

[5]The term "*when* the Alliance as a whole" has subsequently been changed to "*where* the Alliance as a whole." This could be seen as a distinction without a difference, but it has recently become a focus for debate regarding what the term "where" means: a geographic, temporal, or functional term. Also important in terms of later developments was the St. Mâlo call for a "strong and competitive European defence industry and technology." On the issue of NATO's primacy, as recently as Prime Minister Blair's visit to the White House in February 2001, he repeated the formula—with the one "key" word change ("where NATO as a whole is not engaged")—in his effort to offset continuing U.S. criticism. The White House, Office of the Press Secretary, *Remarks by the President and Prime Minister Blair in Joint Press Conference*, Green Top Camp Dining Hall, Camp David, Maryland, February 23, 2001.

vance notice to anyone—and that it was agreed at the summit level, thus giving it more actual political weight than anything else done since Berlin-Brussels on developing ESDI.[6] Indeed, St. Mâlo has acquired more symbolic than substantive significance, but it is nonetheless important. Under the circumstances, it was not surprising that the European Council, meeting at its Vienna summit a week later, did little more than welcome the St. Mâlo declaration, as part of a brief discussion of "the new impetus given to the debate on a common European policy on security and defence." At the same time, the December 1998 Vienna summit's *Presidency Conclusions* (in effect, the "communiqué" of a European Council summit) noted that

> The reinforcement of European solidarity must take into account the various positions of European States, including the obligations of some Member States within NATO.[7]

---

[6]British officials argue that they did apprise the United States in advance of what was going to be agreed upon at St. Mâlo; but certainly it was not well known, and particularly not among those Americans—especially in Congress—who proved to be most concerned about what was agreed upon.

[7]See Vienna European Council, *Presidency Conclusions,* December 11–12, 1998, paragraphs 73–76. The Vienna summit also agreed to appoint as soon as possible a new double-hatted official, secretary general of the European Council and High Representative for CFSP, and that this individual should be "a personality with a strong political profile."

Chapter Six

THE THREE *D*s—AND A FOURTH

Debate was now clearly under way about aspects of ESDI that had not been much discussed in the two years since the Berlin and Brussels agreements. Indeed, it can be argued that much of the ensuing transatlantic disagreement has stemmed precisely from the desultory and almost haphazard way in which the 1996 agreements had been presented in public, on both sides of the Atlantic, and certainly to the U.S. Congress. The agreements were, of course, complex and not easily understood by nonspecialists in the intricacies of either NATO or European Union politics and organization: Even the concept of "separable but not separate" military capabilities is not self-evident and requires explanation. St. Mâlo, however, provided political highlighting, especially for Americans, who were surprised to see Britain and France in agreement on a matter of military security and activities affecting NATO.

At the semiannual NATO foreign ministers' meeting in Brussels on December 8, Secretary of State Madeleine Albright gave the first, quick U.S. response to St. Mâlo. She recalled U.S. support for an ESDI "within the Alliance," and stated that "we enthusiastically support any such measures that enhance European capabilities."[1] But she then set out three standards for judgment—standards that instantly became known as the "three *D*s":

> The key to a successful initiative is to focus on practical military capabilities. Any initiative must avoid preempting Alliance decision-

---

[1]See the text of Secretary Albright's remarks to the North Atlantic Council ministerial meeting, Brussels, December 8, 1998.

making by *de-linking* ESDI from NATO, avoid *duplicating* existing efforts, and avoid *discriminating* against non-EU members [emphasis added].[2]

1. DE-LINKING

The first "D"—*de-linking*—clearly related to the idea of "autonomous" European action introduced in the St. Mâlo declaration, along with the absence of the ritual words "separable but not separate" military capabilities. While not restated on this occasion, the U.S. position was clear: For the United States to agree to the release of NATO assets for WEU use—in major part U.S. assets—the essence of the carefully crafted Berlin-Brussels decisions had to be honored.[3] On this point, the ambiguities of St. Mâlo, coupled with the sudden shift in the British position on ESDI, had led the United States to raise a warning flag.[4]

1+. DECOUPLING

Behind U.S. concern about *de-linking* was also an unstated but long-standing concern within the alliance that, somehow, actions by either the United States or its European allies would lead the security of the two sides of the Atlantic to be *decoupled*. This concept, more

---

[2]Ibid.

[3]Indeed, Albright concluded that "We all agree that we need to finish ESDI *based on the Berlin decisions* by the April [1999] summit" [emphasis added] (ibid.).

[4]The foreign ministers' communiqué on this point was unexceptional, calling for completing the "work on implementing the Berlin and Brussels decisions related to ESDI" by the April 1999 Washington summit, and asking the North Atlantic Council in permanent session "to make recommendations on how best to further enhance the effectiveness of ESDI within the Alliance" (Ministerial Meeting of the North Atlantic Council, *Final Communiqué*, NATO Headquarters, Brussels, NATO Press Release M-NAC-2(98)140, December 8, 1998, paragraph 4. Later, the NATO defense ministers also passed over the issue lightly:

> The fundamental objectives of this [internal] adaptation [of the alliance] are to enhance the Alliance's military effectiveness for the full range of its missions, to preserve the transatlantic link, and to develop the ESDI within the Alliance (Meeting of the North Atlantic Council in Defence Ministers' Session, *Final Communiqué*, Brussels, NATO Press Release M-NAC-D-2(98)152, December 17, 1998, paragraph 13).

political than military and usually expressed in the negative (as the need to "*avoid decoupling*") lay behind the fundamental security arrangements of the cold war and most of the efforts by the United States during that time to demonstrate that it would be prepared to initiate the use of nuclear weapons on the allies' behalf in response to Soviet and Warsaw Pact conventional force aggression against Western Europe. The decoupling issue was also a central feature of allied debate over the Reagan administration's proposal in the 1980s for a Strategic Defense Initiative—with many Europeans worrying that a shield to protect the United States, however imperfectly, against nuclear attack would connote a loss of American willingness to share the same risks as the allies.

This time, however, the shoe was on the other foot: concern in the United States that the European allies taking part in ESDI could create circumstances in which they would see their security as somehow decoupled from the Atlantic framework. Given the relatively small size and limited range of actions that might be undertaken by any European ESDI force—at least as formally presented in the Petersberg Tasks—this risk should have appeared to be minimal. But as a political matter, it gained greater currency in Washington and, rightly or wrongly, has been a source of concern ever since. This is so despite the fact that U.S. speculation about the risks of decoupling posed by ESDI—including St. Mâlo and its aftermath—goes against two clearly positive aspects of ESDI, welcomed by the United States: (1) the Europeans would be doing more for defense and hence for intra-allied burden sharing (however limited);[5] and (2) some European military capacity, not solely bound up in NATO, could actually reassure Europeans of their ability to take some actions in circumstances in which the United States chose not to become engaged. By this argument, ESDI should *reinforce* European confidence in U.S. commitments to European security and thus the political and military *coupling* of the two sides of the Atlantic.

---

[5]The French defense minister has argued that

> the prime objective of the common European security and defence policy is to strengthen our military capabilities so that Europeans can make a greater contribution to the security of their continent, within the Alliance framework, or within the EU (Alain Richard, French Minister of Defense, *Speech to the "Wehrkunde,"* Munich, February 3, 2001, www.france.diplomatie.fr/ europe/politique/defense/richard030201.gb.html.

2. DISCRIMINATING

Discrimination against non-EU members was more tangible but not central, at least then, to the underlying debate about NATO-WEU relations. At the time of St. Mâlo, five members of NATO—Canada, Iceland, Norway, Turkey, and the United States—were not EU members, and now, with the addition to NATO of the Czech Republic, Hungary, and Poland, there are eight. Furthermore, despite its eligibility, Denmark had chosen not to become a full member of WEU. Would any or all of these states be able to take part in WEU military operations? The issue was most pertinent in regard to Turkey, which was struggling to be accepted as a potential member of the European Union and was still, by the time of the St. Mâlo declaration, being kept firmly outside the gate. At the Helsinki EU summit a year later, it was finally put on the list of countries that would be "destined to join the Union"—although, of course, "on the basis of the same criteria as applied to the other candidate States."[6]

At one level, this issue of participation by NATO non-WEU members should not have emerged: After all, as a necessary condition of releasing any NATO assets for use by WEU, the North Atlantic Council would first have to approve it, by consensus, and Turkey has a veto. Further, lest Turkey be put under intense pressure by the Europeans in the council, the United States had promised to stand with it on this matter. In addition, NATO's Berlin-Brussels agreements specifically provided for "the development, with the participation of all European Allies, of the ESDI within the Alliance;"[7] and it had already been agreed that the non-EU members of NATO could take part in various aspects of WEU activities, including planning, by being "able

---

[6]See Helsinki European Council, *Presidency Conclusions*, December 10–11, 1999, paragraph 12:

> The European Council welcomes recent positive developments in Turkey as noted in the Commission's progress report, as well as its intention to continue its reforms towards complying with the Copenhagen criteria. Turkey is a candidate State destined to join the Union on the basis of the same criteria as applied to the other candidate States. Building on the existing European strategy, Turkey, like other candidate States, will benefit from a pre-accession strategy to stimulate and support its reforms.

[7]Meeting of the North Atlantic Council in Defence Ministers' Session, June 13, 1996, op. cit., paragraph 8.

to be associated to the [WEU] Planning Cell [set up by the Petersberg Declaration of June 1992] through a permanent liaison arrangement." Also, "they will take part on the same basis as full members in WEU military operations to which they commit forces."[8] Thus the U.S. introduction of this "*D*" after St. Mâlo was designed to underscore a substantive point, especially in view of one underlying idea of ESDI: It is about increasing the storehouse of European security, writ large, by creating a capacity for EU states to have a Common Foreign and Security Policy and a defense component able to respond to CFSP decisions, at least regarding Petersberg Tasks.

At another level, however, there has developed more serious concern regarding circumstances in which military actions would be taken within the ESDI framework but *without* calling upon NATO assets— as, obviously, would be the right of the WEU/EU, without let or hindrance from NATO or any of the allied states. This matter was certainly brought into play by the introduction, at St. Mâlo and afterward, of the idea that the new European construction should have the capacity to take *autonomous* action. But would non-EU NATO members be able to take part in WEU operations under these conditions? In theory, that point had already been settled in the Maastricht Treaty:

---

[8]WEU Council of Ministers, June 19, 1992, op. cit., paragraph III.B. The planning arrangement (precisely for Iceland, Norway, and Turkey) was later expanded, so they

> may nominate officers to the Planning Cell in order to increase WEU's planning capabilities and to enable WEU to draw more easily on the Associate Members' expertise and resources for the tasks identified in the Petersberg Declaration" (WEU Council of Ministers, *Kirchberg Declaration*, "III. Declaration Following on from the 'Document on Associate Membership' of 20 November 1992," Luxembourg, May 9, 1994).

See also Document on Associate Members of WEU of the Republic of Iceland, the Kingdom of Norway and the Republic of Turkey, November 20, 1992:

> [The associate members] will be able to participate in their implementation [i.e., decisions made by member states] unless a majority of the member States, or half of the member States including the Presidency, decide otherwise.

> [Non-EU] European Member States of NATO are invited to become associate members of WEU in a way which will give them *the possibility to participate fully in the activities of WEU* [emphasis added].[9]

The issue has since been reopened, especially because ESDP has seemed to become more of a reality. In one form or another, virtually all of the NATO states that do not belong to the EU have made clear their concerns about being sidelined in the event of a military action within the framework of ESDP. And because it is not yet clear to what extent the EU—e.g., through the projected Headline Goal Task Force—will in fact want to draw upon NATO assets, even while the Europeans express a desire to be capable of *autonomous* action, discrimination against non-EU members is still a salient matter within NATO and in its relations with the EU. Nor is this just about the interests of the affected non-EU NATO countries (plus Denmark): It also relates to the abiding sense within NATO of shared experience, shared risks, and a shared political-strategic perspective.

It is important to dwell a bit further on the case of Turkey. For most of the non-EU members of NATO, participation in ESDP has seemed a second-order matter, especially since they have not had major expectations for it, at least in the short to medium term, except in regard to the process of developing European integration.[10] Turkey's problem has a more important character. As ESDI-ESDP has developed beyond the necessary reliance on NATO assets and Turkey's potential veto, the issue by 2000 became whether Turkey would be able to take part in the full range of discussions and decisions within EU institutions, leading from the onset of a crisis to the actual use of

---

[9]See *Maastricht Declarations*, December 10, 1991. Note that Canada is not covered by this phrase: A point that would later acquire significance for Ottawa.

[10]To be sure, there was some effort by EU members to take advantage of the anomalous situation of differential memberships. Thus, Norway has at times been put under considerable pressure by some of the Europeans to "buy EU" in terms of defense goods—including high-performance aircraft. The argument made is that, because of its rejection of EU membership by referenda (1972 and 1994), Norway would lack access to Brussels institutions for purposes of influencing decisions by which, because of its membership in the European Economic Area, Norway would be bound even though it had no role in shaping these decisions. Showing favoritism to European arms suppliers has been represented as a way for Norway to be accorded some influence via the route of ESDP. "All is fair" in the arms trade as in other aspects of international life! Comments made to the author by various Norwegian government representatives, January 2000.

force to achieve one Petersberg Task or another. The topic arose as late as the Washington summit of April 1999, even though the alliance's new Strategic Concept was quite clear:

> [The allies were prepared to] make [NATO's] assets and capabilities available for operations in which the Alliance is not engaged militarily under the political control and strategic direction either of the WEU or as otherwise agreed, *taking into account the full participation of all European Allies if they were so to choose* [emphasis added].[11]

Furthermore, the June 1999 European Council summit at Cologne set the goal of developing

> an effective EU-led crisis management in which NATO members, as well as neutral and non-allied members of the EU, can participate *fully and on an equal footing* in the EU operations [emphasis added]; . . . [and arrangements made would] allow non-EU European allies and partners to take part to the fullest possible extent in this endeavour.[12]

However, an element of ambiguity (or at least confusion) was also introduced, from the point of view of Turkey and similarly situated non-EU NATO members, when the EU endorsed a report that made clear that

> *The Council of the European Union would . . . be able to take decisions* on the whole range of political, economic, and military in-

---

[11]See NATO, *The Alliance's Strategic Concept, Approved by the Heads of State and Government Participating in the Meeting of the North Atlantic Council in Washington, D.C., on 23rd and 24th April 1999,* Release NAC-S(99)65, April 24, 1999, paragraph 30. Furthermore the document states that, regarding the EU's "efforts to strengthen its security and defence dimension, . . . all European Allies should be involved in it, building on arrangements developed by NATO and the WEU" (ibid., paragraph 17).

[12]Cologne European Council, *Presidency Conclusions,* June 3–4, 1999, "Annex III, European Council Declaration on Strengthening the Common European Policy on Security and Defence," paragraph 3. It can be noted that these formulations did not use the designators "the" or "all" to modify "NATO members," and "non-EU European allies." But to isolate Turkey on that basis would be a lawyer's quibble.

struments at its disposal when responding to crisis situations [emphasis added].[13]

Thus, the Cologne summit text contained a critical distinction:

> [While ensuring] that all participants in an EU-led operation will have equal rights in respect to the conduct of that operation, . . . [this would be] without prejudice to the principle of the EU's decisionmaking autonomy, notably the right of the Council to discuss and decide matters of principle and policy.[14]

When it became clear that Turkey would not have full access to this process, in December 2000 it placed a hold on further work between NATO and the EU on defining security relations between the two institutions. The EU could argue that it was not being ambiguous, but merely hair-splitting: "Participants in an EU-led operation" might have equal rights; but they would not become "participants" until relevant decisions had already been made by the European Council. This has proved to be the nub of the problem.

For the United States, this matter regarding Turkey might be seen as a problem only in two respects: its relationship with Turkey (and aspirations to see it play a full role in Western security institutions and eventually become a member of the EU); and the U.S. desire to see NATO gain as much as possible from the EU in terms of arrangements that would keep ESDP from eroding NATO prerogatives. However, as the Turkish hold on formal agreements continued, a further and more important U.S. concern developed: The EU might forge ahead with its own developments, potentially widening the political and psychological gap with NATO, perhaps more by inadvertence than by design.

3. DUPLICATING

At least at the time of St. Mâlo (December 1998), the most important and most tangible of the three (or four) U.S. "*D*s" was duplication. On the face of it, Secretary Albright's injunction "to avoid duplicating

---

[13]Ibid., paragraph 2.
[14]Ibid., paragraph 5.

existing efforts" was simply a U.S. plea for the Europeans, in crafting ESDI, not to spend scarce resources on trying to create a second set of capabilities that they could just as easily obtain from NATO, on the basis of the 1996 grand bargain. Given that the military budgets of most European states were in fact decreasing (see Table 1), this was not an idle matter: Indeed, trying to avoid unnecessary duplication (beyond, say, the WEU's having the machinery needed to provide it with the capacity to make decisions, to incorporate basic strategic planning,[15] and to exercise essential command and control) had been a major reason for creating ESDI within NATO, using NATO assets, rather than outside it: the principle of "separable but not separate" military capabilities. It seemed to the United States—and also to most military and budgetary experts—to make little sense to try creating a second set of military goods (especially expensive hardware) simply to be able to designate one set as "NATO" and the other as "WEU." This was especially true since, as noted earlier, neither NATO nor the WEU (and its EU successor, the Headline Goal Task Force) in effect "owns" very much of this hardware, but rather calls upon national contributions when deciding to undertake a military operation.[16]

Of course, most U.S. analysts also judged that the WEU was not in fact very likely, by itself, to take any military action of any major size: They presumed that any substantial military challenge would also engage the United States, and thus, under the implicit concept of

---

[15]The WEU has long had its own planning cell. Following the Berlin-Brussels decisions, however, NATO has undertaken major responsibility for WEU planning, including the creation of a joint planning staff for CJTF headquarters. See Ministerial Meeting of the North Atlantic Council, June 13, 1996, op. cit., paragraph 6:

> We have also instructed the NATO Military Authorities to develop the terms of reference of the Combined Joint Planning Staff which would perform centralized CJTF headquarters planning functions and co-ordination with all relevant headquarters, as well as with forces that might serve under a CJTF headquarters, and as appropriate with the WEU Planning Cell.

As discussed below, just where ESDP operational planning will take place has been a major issue in its relations with NATO.

[16]Even the EU's project Headline Goal Task Force would consist largely of forces that could as easily find themselves employed in NATO-run military actions as EU-run actions.

Table 1

Allied Defense Spending, 1990–2000
(1995 prices and exchange rates)

Country	Currency	1990	1995	1996	1997	1998	1999	2000[a]	%-1	%-2
Belgium	Francs	175534	131156	129190	127803	127260	128577	129266	-25.3	0.5
Czech Rep.	Koruny	—	—	—	—	—	31339	32682	—	4.3
Denmark	Kroner	18453	17468	17426	17611	17647	17498	16952	-5.3	-3.1
France	Francs	257575	238432	233988	234643	227824	230108	232613	-7.4	1.1
Germany	DMs	80901	58986	58076	56573	56699	57618	57033	-27.1	-1.0
Greece	Drachma	1177417	1171377	1250955	1318338	1435153	1495834	1562216	-0.5	4.4
Hungary	Forint	—	—	—	—	—	106469	115143	—	8.1
Italy	1000 Lire	35783	31561	31790	31458	32206	32902	32305	-11.8	-1.8
Luxembourg	Francs	3734	4194	4341	4650	4985	5083	5117	12.3	0.7
Netherlands	Guilders	15158	12864	13068	12967	12817	13424	12759	-15.1	-5.0
Norway	Kroner	23842	22224	22454	22117	23578	23393	22890	-90.7	-2.2
Poland	Zlotys	—	—	—	—	—	7770	7949	—	2.3
Portugal	Escudos	393237	403478	390055	399040	381430	403191	403191	2.6	2.5
Spain	Peseta	1201473	1078751	1055100	1062949	1040030	1047385	1109069	-10.2	5.9
Turkey	1000 Liras	273695	302864	323744	340749	353579	370788	419222	10.7	13.1
UK	Pounds	28008	21439	21537	20242	20510	20123	19910	-23.5	-1.1

Table 1—continued

Country	Currency	1990	1995	1996	1997	1998	1999	2000[a]	%-1	%-2
Europe	**US $**	**220294**	**184352**	**183737**	**181236**	**181479**	**188818**	**189741**	**-16.3**	**—**
Canada	Dollars	14708	12457	11330	10574	11507	11932	11211	-15.3	-6.0
U.S.	Dollars	354956	278856	265599	263805	256667	258348	266762	-21.4	3.3
North Am.	**US $**	**365673**	**287933**	**273854**	**275510**	**265051**	**267042**	**274931**	**-21.3**	
Total	**US $**	**585767**	**472284**	**457591**	**452746**	**446530**	**455861**	**464672**	**-19.4**	

NOTES: "%-1" is the percentage change from 1990 to 1995 spending. "%-2" is the percentage change from 1999 to 2000 spending.
[a]2000 figures are estimates.

SOURCE: NATO, *Tables on Total Defence Expenditures and Defence Expenditure Annual Volume Change*, Press Release M-DPC-2 (2000) 107, December 5, 2000.

"NATO first"—at least as understood by the United States—the locus for decision and action would naturally shift to the alliance. As a result, any significant duplication of effort, with serious resource implications, would not contribute much in practice to meeting European security goals—which, by this logic, would almost always be shared by the United States. Nevertheless, the issue of "unnecessary duplication" has continued to be at the center of transatlantic debate about the future of ESDI-ESDP and its relationship to NATO.

Chapter Seven

DEFENSE CAPABILITIES AND THE DEFENSE CAPABILITIES INITIATIVE

One significant way in which the duplication issue has remained important emerged from the introduction of another factor. By the time of St. Mâlo and the first U.S. formal response to it, the NATO Alliance was also "seized of" concerns about its own military resources and capacities. Having successfully completed the design phase of adapting the NATO Alliance to meet the challenges of the post–cold war era,[1] the allied states had to consider the scope of possible NATO military actions in the future and, in particular, the capabilities needed to undertake such actions. These concerns arose even before the alliance decided, beyond generalities, upon potential areas for military action (other than requirements that could arise under the Washington Treaty's Article 5) or the geographic limits of such action. The need to give reality to alliance "adaptation"—in this case creating the appropriate military capabilities—begged those questions, which remain unresolved.

But the allies did understand, in general, that a renovated NATO Alliance would need to maintain a significant level of military capabilities and that individual nation's armed forces would need to undergo modernization, simply to achieve the indispensable goal that the alliance should continue, along with its integrated military com-

---

[1]See, for instance, Ambassador Robert E. Hunter, *Speech at Latvian Institute of International Affairs, Riga,* Latvia, December 9, 1995, www.usis.bkc.lv/archives/documents/hunter.htm; and Robert E. Hunter, "NATO's Role in Bosnia and the New European Security Framework," *Oxford International Review,* Vol. VII, No. 2, Spring 1996.

mand structure and the ability of the military forces of different allied states to fight effectively together. At the very least, some minimal level of defense capabilities was necessary to keep the alliance viable. But stress on creating serious military capabilities came especially from the United States, primarily on three scores. One—which in fact proved to be the least important of the three—was prompted by NATO's decision to admit three new members, with the prospect of admitting still more. The debate on NATO enlargement, especially within the U.S. Congress, focused to a considerable degree on military questions that might not otherwise have arisen: Would NATO be able to honor its new commitments and how much would it cost? Would the United States have to bear the brunt of the new commitments, or would allied forces also step up to the mark? And what would be the future of the alliance—including its military future—into which new allies would be entering?

A second factor leading the United States to focus on pressing for the creation of serious NATO military capabilities for the future was the belief that, should the alliance be called upon to act militarily, it would be more likely to take place outside the alliance's traditional sphere of action rather than inside. Geographically, this could still be in "Europe," a concept clearly embracing the Former Yugoslavia and the Balkans, generally; but it could also extend to regions beyond. In part, this assessment recalled what allies had been required to do, without warning, in the Persian Gulf in 1990–91; in part it reflected concerns about other potential sources of tension and conflict affecting Western interests beyond the Mediterranean and well into the western part of Asia.[2] Indeed, there has been a running debate within the alliance on this point, highlighted by Secretary Albright's presentation to the December 1997 NATO foreign ministers' meeting—"Our nations share global interests";[3] by more limited expecta-

---

[2] European discussions of the Petersburg Tasks have presumed the possibility of military action beyond the European continent, but this has almost always related to actions such as rescuing civilians from conflict situations and other low-level military operations. The one geographic area where the Europeans might get involved military, where the United States (and hence NATO) might stand aloof is presumed to be North Africa and parts of sub-Saharan Africa, especially francophone countries.

[3] Continuing the quote: "that require us to work together with the same degree of solidarity that we have long maintained on this continent" (Secretary of State Albright, North Atlantic Council Ministerial Meeting, Brussels, December 16, 1997).

tions she expressed a year later;[4] and by an uneasy compromise reached at the April 1999 Washington summit where, in their revision to the NATO Strategic Concept, the allies agreed only that "Alliance security must . . . take account of the global context. Alliance security interests can be affected by . . . risks of a wider nature."[5]

Third and most important, the United States, more than any other ally, was concerned that the differential pace of military modernization within the alliance risked rendering the various allies less capable of working and fighting together. At the most practical level, this difference in pace had become apparent during military operations in Bosnia, especially in areas such as communications and sustainability of military operations.[6] The point was reinforced later, and

---

[4]Secretary Albright's remarks to the North Atlantic Council Ministerial Meeting, Brussels, December 8, 1998:

> [T]here are those who try to suggest that . . . by talking about common Euro-Atlantic interests beyond collective defense, we are somehow tinkering with the original intent of the North Atlantic Treaty. . . . I will repeat it again today: this is hogwash. . . . We are neither altering the North Atlantic Treaty, nor attempting to create some kind of a new "global" NATO. What we are doing is using the flexibility the Treaty always offered to adapt this Alliance to the realities of a new strategic environment and the challenges we must face together in the twenty-first century.

[5]In particular:

> The security of the Alliance remains subject to a wide variety of military and non-military risks which are multi-directional and often difficult to predict. These risks include uncertainty and instability in and around the Euro-Atlantic area and the possibility of regional crises at the periphery of the Alliance, which could evolve rapidly. Some countries in and around the Euro-Atlantic area face serious economic, social and political difficulties. Ethnic and religious rivalries, territorial disputes, inadequate or failed efforts at reform, the abuse of human rights, and the dissolution of states can lead to local and even regional instability. The resulting tensions could lead to crises affecting Euro-Atlantic stability, to human suffering, and to armed conflicts. Such conflicts could affect the security of the Alliance by spilling over into neighboring countries, including NATO countries, or in other ways, and could also affect the security of other states.

See NATO, April 24, 1999, op. cit., paragraph 20.

[6]See Secretary of Defense William S. Cohen, *Remarks at the Transatlantic Forum of the Western European Union*, Washington, D.C., June 30, 1998:

> First, we need to really improve the interoperability of our forces. . . . In the early days of the deployment to Bosnia, we had great difficulty communicating with one another because we had incompatible equipment. . . . [F]orces

much more intensely, during the Kosovo conflict. Furthermore, with its global reach, the United States had a clear incentive to continue modernizing its military forces, and it was embarking on its Revolution in Military Affairs and other efforts, with an accent on taking advantage of a wide range of technological advances in sensors, computation, communication, and the capacity effectively to integrate and act upon great quantities of information.[7] This has included spending sums on military research and development that are more than triple the comparable spending by the rest of the NATO allies combined.

To be sure, the issue of "interoperability" had bedeviled the Atlantic Alliance almost since its inception; but the problem is arguably more serious in the post–cold war environment, at least in terms of relations among militaries if not also in terms of the stakes involved, because of the rate at which U.S. military capabilities have been diverging from those of most other allies. Furthermore, in the most likely kinds of warfare in the future, coordination among the forces of different allies will have to be broader, deeper, and more comprehensive than would have been true in the notional European conflict of the cold war. Then, allied forces connected with one another largely at the level of divisions or corps, not companies and platoons, and without today's accent on integrating forces in air, land, sea, and space in "real time" and otherwise putting such heavy reliance on a common base of information technology in all of NATO's key military applications. This coordination would be important particularly in two areas: peacekeeping within Europe (as in the former Yugoslavia), or coalition operations outside of Europe (so far not agreed to within the alliance, but a major U.S. aspiration).

---

still need to share more information and data more efficiently. So one of our goals has to be to improve our ability to communicate, not through a complete commonality of equipment, but through the compatibility of overall systems. Second, we need to enhance our ability to sustain the operations of our deployed forces. Again, Bosnia reminds us that operations can last for a long period of time and they can challenge even the best-prepared logistics pipelines. . . . So we have to ensure that our forces are backed up by the most advanced logistics supply systems in a seamless flow of critical information between those in the supply lines and troops on the front lines.

[7]The term "C^{3}ISR"—command, control, communications, intelligence, surveillance, and reconnaissance—captured a major part of these developments.

With these considerations very much in mind, the United States proposed, and the allies agreed to, a new "initiative on defence capabilities" at the December 1998 NATO defense ministers' meeting, focusing in particular on technology and interoperability, in all the areas "which are critical to the successful execution of joint military operations."[8] This program and a framework for action were formally adopted at the April 1999 Washington summit, which also set up a High-Level Steering Group to foster its implementation within the alliance.[9]

> DCI aims in particular to improve alliance capabilities in the following five, overlapping areas:

> • "Mobility and deployability": i.e., the ability to deploy forces quickly to where they are needed, including areas outside alliance territory.

> • "Sustainability": i.e., the ability to maintain and supply forces far from their home bases and to ensure that sufficient fresh forces are available for long-duration operations.

---

[8]See Meeting of the North Atlantic Council in Defence Ministers' Session, December 17, 1998, op. cit., paragraph 20:

> To support the ability of the Alliance to undertake the full range of its missions, work has been set in train to develop proposals for an initiative on defence capabilities which could be adopted at the Washington Summit. Building on progress to date, such an initiative could aim at developing a common assessment of requirements for the full range of military operations and, with a particular emphasis on technology and interoperability, especially in such areas as logistics and command, control and communications, address capabilities which are critical to the successful execution of joint military operations, such as readiness, deployability, mobility, sustainability, survivability, and effective engagement.

An unspoken but critical subtext is the U.S. desire that NATO be able to undertake coalition operations beyond Europe.

[9]See *Defence Capabilities Initiative*, NATO Press Release NAC-S(99)69, April 25, 1999.

> The Group, which is made up of senior officials from national capitals and chaired by the Deputy Secretary General, meets every few weeks to review progress and guide the process ("NATO's Defence Capabilities Initiative," *NATO Fact Sheet*, August 9, 2000, www.nato.int/docu/facts/2000/nato-dci.htm).

- "Effective engagement": i.e., the ability to successfully engage an adversary in all types of operations, from high to low intensity.

- "Survivability": i.e., the ability to protect forces and infrastructure against current and future threats.

- "Interoperable communications": i.e., command, control, and information systems that are compatible with each other, to enable forces from different countries to work effectively together.[10]

This Defense Capabilities Initiative (DCI) was not created because of debate on ESDI, although that was clearly a factor in terms of its design, along with all other potential needs for NATO forces. But for the United States, developing these capabilities for military effectiveness—both for "power projection" and to preserve a functioning military alliance in an environment of rapid (and differential) technological change in allied militaries—was far more important than preparing to help the Europeans in their efforts to advance integration in the field of foreign policy and defense. Yet the link was there—as Secretary Albright had said at NATO soon after the St. Mâlo declaration: "The key to a successful [European Security and Defense Initiative] is to focus on practical military capabilities."[11] Indeed, allied progress—meaning the Europeans' progress—on DCI has remained a touchstone of U.S. judgments about the worth of ESDP and, conversely, the risks it could, in Washington's judgment, pose to the effectiveness of the Atlantic Alliance.

Furthermore, of the several dozen items that have come to be the basic list of DCI items for action, some at the top can be said to be of a "double duty" quality: notably in strategic air- and sealift.[12] It would

---

[10]See also "NATO on Defense Capabilities Initiative," *NATO Fact Sheet*, April 24, 1999, Washington NATO summit web site (www.fas.org/man/nato/natodocs/99042408.htm).

[11]Text of Secretary Albright's remarks to the North Atlantic Council ministerial meeting, Brussels, December 8, 1998.

[12]See, for instance, Defence Planning Committee and the Nuclear Planning Group, *Final Communiqué*, Press Communiqué M-DPC/NPG-2(2000)115, December 5, 2000; and European Council Summit, *Presidency Report on the European Security and*

be possible for the United States to argue that for the Europeans to build their own large air transport (the "Future Large Aircraft," or A400M) would not be a good use of resources—both because of industrial inefficiencies and the availability of U.S. aircraft (C-17, C-130J), or even the Ukrainian *Antonov* AN-124, which could roughly provide whatever capabilities the Europeans would need. Nevertheless, the U.S. argument against "unnecessary duplication" would also have to be measured against the political and industrial-based goals of European states, as well as against the possibility that, if there were no indigenous European airlift candidate, perhaps the ESDP states would simply divert the money to nondefense spending.[13] Within reason, this has been the European trump card on the issue of "duplication." As discussed earlier, a major motive for the United States' turnaround on the idea of having a viable "European pillar" within the alliance was that this could provide a political incentive for creating defense capabilities that would otherwise not likely exist, for lack of domestic political support. Like democracy itself, processes in democratic states of creating defense capabilities cannot be held up as models of "efficiency."

Defense Policy, Nice, December 2000, paragraph I (1). Relating NATO DCI goals to those of ESDI—including the Headline Goal Task Force decided upon at the December 1999 Helsinki European Council—has been a critical problem. Thus, U.S. Defense Secretary William Cohen told the 36th Munich Conference on Security Policy in February 2000 that

> NATO members and other participants in the EU's Common Foreign and Security Policy need to turn their program priorities—*which, importantly, are largely identical and compatible with the DCI areas*—into concrete and achievable goals [emphasis added] (U.S. Department of Defense, February 7, 2000).

[13]The United States would also need to reinforce—beyond the commitments made at the time of the Berlin-Brussels "grand bargain"—the point that U.S. strategic lift aircraft would indeed be made available to the EU through ESDP, even in circumstances far afield and of relatively low strategic interest to the United States—e.g., parts of Africa.

Chapter Eight

FROM WASHINGTON TO COLOGNE

Following the St. Mâlo summit, the pace picked up in bargaining between NATO and the WEU states over the nature of their relationship. The key focus was at NATO's Washington summit in April 1999, where the allies "acknowledged" the EU's "resolve," post–St. Mâlo, "to have the capacity for *autonomous action* so that it can take decisions and approve military action *where the alliance as a whole is not engaged* [emphasis added in both places]."[1] NATO's new Strategic Concept agreed that ESDI "will continue to be developed within NATO."[2] And this process

> will assist the European Allies to act by themselves as required through the readiness of the Alliance, on a case-by-case basis and by consensus, to make its assets and capabilities available for operations in which the Alliance is not engaged militarily under the political control and strategic direction either of the WEU or as otherwise agreed[3]

What this meant in practice was spelled out in the Washington summit communiqué, again presuming that ESDI would be built "within the Alliance,"[4] including to help

---

[1] NATO, *Washington Summit Communiqué*, Press Release NAC-S(99)64, April 24, 1999, paragraph 9.

[2] In the context of the ongoing debate, it should be recalled that 10 of the 19 Allies that subscribed to this document were full members of the WEU, including France, the most active proponent of "autonomous action" for what would emerge as ESDP.

[3] NATO, *The Alliance's Strategic Concept*, April 24, 1999, op. cit., paragraph 30.

[4] NATO, *Washington Summit Communiqué*, April 24, 1999, op. cit., paragraph 4.

both EU members and other European Allies to take the necessary steps to strengthen their defence capabilities, especially for new missions, avoiding unnecessary duplication.[5]

The NATO allies—by implication, featuring the United States—also took a step well beyond their earlier work in developing a relationship of trust and confidence with ESDI by stating their readiness to

> adopt the necessary arrangements for *ready access* by the European Union to the collective assets and capabilities of the Alliance, for operations in which the Alliance as a whole is not engaged militarily as an Alliance. The [North Atlantic] Council in Permanent Session will approve these arrangements, *which will respect the requirements of NATO operations and the coherence of its command structure* [emphasis added in both places].[6]

At this point, NATO also acknowledged that the European agent for operating ESDI would be the EU rather than the WEU, and it endorsed two points of particular concern to some Europeans and especially France: Arrangements worked out would "address"—i.e., make provisions for—

> *Assured* EU access to NATO planning capabilities able to contribute to military planning for EU-led operations; [and] . . . *the presumption* of availability to the EU of pre-identified NATO capabilities and common assets for use in EU-led operations [emphasis added in both places].[7]

This new arrangement—or modified bargain—between NATO and ESDI came be called *Berlin-plus,* in that it reaffirmed NATO's primacy in terms of actual military action, acknowledged that there would be no "unnecessary duplication," restated (by implication) the

---

[5]Ibid., paragraph 9.

[6]Ibid.

[7]Ibid. This arrangement went on to provide:

> Identification of a range of European command options for EU-led operations, further developing the role of Deputy SACEUR in order for him to assume fully and effectively his European responsibilities, [and] . . . the further adaptation of NATO's defence planning system to incorporate more comprehensively the availability of forces for EU-led operation.

"separable but not separate" military capabilities principle, insisted that non-EU NATO members be engaged, and repeated several times that the EU would operate only where NATO forces were not engaged militarily. In return, NATO accepted the notion of "autonomous [EU] action," although without precisely defining what that term meant, and increased the chances that NATO would not try to undercut the deal in the midst of a crisis, by adding the words "assured" (access to NATO planning) and "presumption" (of access to NATO capabilities and assets).[8]

There the debate might have come to rest, had it not been for what happened a little over a month later, when the European Council met at the head of state and government level at Cologne (June 3–4, 1999). In the interim, the EU's four main reasons for promoting ESDI-ESDP—to further European integration, to accommodate France's competition with Germany, to recognize that the Franco-American deal on France's reintegration into NATO's integrated command structure had failed to reach completion, and to provide Britain with something to show its European allegiance—had been joined by a fifth reason: the growing sense in Europe that it had not been able to "pull its weight" in the air war then being conducted against Serbia in the Kosovo conflict.[9] This fact raised three principle issues: the short-fall in European high-technology military capabilities; the renewal, however restrained, of American rumblings about "burden sharing"; and irritation in many European capitals (and among some European militaries) that the United States had been calling most of the shots in the conflict, sometimes a bit heavy-handedly.[10] Indeed, the added impetus to ESDP for many Europeans

---

[8]For the proponents of EU activities under ESDP that do not rely on the principle of building capabilities within NATO, "separable but not separate" from it, these two points are considered the essence of Berlin-plus.

[9]Thus, NATO Secretary General Lord Robertson noted that:

> Collectively, the European members of NATO spend almost two-thirds of the United States' defense budget—but Kosovo made it clear they have nothing like two-thirds of the real capability of the U.S. (NATO, Parliamentary Assembly, *Press Statement*, Amsterdam, November 15, 1999).

[10]This grumbling had its American analogue: The lack of sufficient European capacity to keep pace with U.S. technology meant that the United States had to assume an even greater share of the air campaign, and that some European air assets could not even be employed because they lacked the capability, for instance, to communicate by

was less about being able to do more, but rather to have more of a say in what decisions about security and the use of force were being made, even within NATO.[11]

In any event, the *Presidency Conclusions* of the Cologne summit addressed in depth the issue of "the common European policy on security and defense." In particular, it noted that the European Council

> should have the ability to take decisions on the full range of conflict prevention and crisis management tasks defined in the Treaty on European Union, the "Petersberg Tasks." . . . [This meant] the Union must have the capacity for autonomous action, backed up by credible military forces, the means to decide to use them, and a readiness to do so, in order to respond to international crises without prejudice to actions by NATO.[12]

However, as the U.S. in particular was quick to note, this statement—along with the companion report from the German EU presidency—was selective in what part of the new Berlin-plus bargain struck at Washington to endorse. At Cologne, emphasis was placed in particular on the NATO summit's words on "assured EU access to NATO planning capabilities able to contribute to military planning for EU-led operations"; and on "the presumption of availability to the EU of pre-identified NATO capabilities and common assets for use in EU-led operations."[13] But the ritual words that would implicitly or explicitly acknowledge NATO's primacy were noticeably absent. There was nothing about building ESDI/ESDP within NATO, about acting only where NATO was not engaged, about protecting the requirements of NATO action or the coherence of the command chain, or about avoiding unnecessary duplication. There were, however, pro-

---

secure channels. The sharpness of some of these U.S. criticisms can be credited with furthering some Europeans' desire to have a capability that would be less subjected to such criticism. Of course, a remedy also lay in simply increasing defense spending, including on "open architecture" equipment that would increase allied interoperability with U.S. forces—whether for operations limited to Europe or for coalition deployments elsewhere.

[11]The argument that the Kosovo experience was the decisive European motive for pursuing ESDP is belied by the fact that much of what has been done antedated that conflict.

[12]Cologne European Council, June 3–4, 1999, op. cit., paragraph 1.

[13]Ibid., paragraph 4.

visions for involving non-EU NATO members. One phrase in the Cologne document—"in order to respond to international crises *without prejudice to actions by NATO*" [emphasis added]—almost seemed to be a deliberate effort to evade the formulation for NATO's role ("where the Alliance as a whole is not engaged," etc.) that had been so carefully worked out for the Washington summit.[14]

It is not surprising that the U.S. administration concluded that the European Union had broken trust over this issue.[15] Notably, in a talk—much discussed in Europe—at the Royal Institute of International Affairs in London, Deputy Secretary of State Strobe Talbott expressed U.S. government fears:

---

[14]Annex III to the *Presidency Conclusions* (Cologne European Council, June 3–4, 1999, op. cit.) did provide for "the need to ensure the development of effective mutual consultation, cooperation and transparency between NATO and the EU." The *Presidency Conclusions* to the Cologne summit also contained an important section on the steps the EU would need to take so that its new venture would be effective, including the need for

> a capacity for analysis of situations, sources of intelligence, and a capability for relevant strategic planning. This may require in particular:
>
> - regular (or ad hoc) meetings of the General Affairs Council, as appropriate including Defense ministers;
>
> - a permanent body in Brussels (Political and Security Committee) consisting of representatives with pol/mil expertise;
>
> - an EU Military Committee consisting of Military Representatives making recommendations to the Political and Security Committee;
>
> - an EU Military Staff including a Situation Centre;
>
> - other resources such as a Satellite Centre, Institute for Security Studies (ibid., paragraph 3).

[15]One European explanation—which did not gain adherents in Washington—was that the Cologne documents were hastily prepared and thus reflected inefficiency as opposed to an effort to undercut the Washington summit agreement. Given the nature of the communiqué-drafting process, however—especially with the close attention always paid by countries like France and Britain, this is not a convincing explanation. For developments during this period, through the December 1999 EU summit, see Karen Donfried and Paul Gallis, *European Security: The Debate in NATO and the European Union*, Congressional Research Service (CRS) Report to Congress, April 25, 2000.

[The United States] would not want to see an ESDI that comes into being first within NATO but then grows out of NATO and finally grows away from NATO, since that would lead to an ESDI that initially duplicates but that could eventually compete with NATO.[16]

---

[16]See U.S. State Department, *Washington File,* October 7, 1999.

CONGRESS RESPONDS

Cologne also reinforced growing skepticism on Capitol Hill about ESDP. The skepticism grew from a compound of several factors, of which the following were most important: (1) poor understanding of what had actually been happening, at Berlin in 1996 and afterward—indeed, the U.S. administration can be faulted for inadequate efforts to see that ESDI issues were well understood in the Congress; (2) concern both about NATO's primacy and the willingness of allies to produce increased military capabilities, including for use beyond Europe; (3) what many members of Congress regarded as the disproportionate share of the military burden borne by the United States during the Kosovo conflict that, at the time, was just ending; and (4) an underlying sense—though rarely articulated—that somehow Europeans (and particularly the French) were seeking to erode American strategic and political influence in Europe.

Thus in November 1999, both Houses of Congress adopted nonbinding resolutions that included strong statements on the ESDI issue. The House resolution (adopted 278 to 133) focused on "shortfalls" in alliance capabilities and the need for "equitable sharing" of defense spending and "capability-building" and stressed that:

> to preserve the solidarity and effectiveness that has been achieved within the Alliance over the last 50 years, it is essential that security arrangements elaborated under the EU's Common Foreign and Security Policy (CFSP) complement, rather than duplicate NATO efforts and institutions, and be linked to, rather than decoupled from NATO structures, and provide for full and active involvement

of all European Allies rather than discriminating against European Allies that are not members of the EU.[1]

For its part, the Senate adopted a resolution that was both stronger and more direct. While it "acknowledge[d] the resolve of the European Union to have the capacity for autonomous action so that it can take decisions and approve military action where the Alliance as a whole is not engaged," [this] "sense of the Senate" resolution presented, without ambiguity, eight clear standards for judgment that ran the gamut of U.S. concerns. In summary:

1. The EU should make it clear that it would undertake "an autonomous mission . . . only after [NATO] had declined to undertake that mission."

2. "Improved European military capabilities, not new institutions outside of the Alliance, are the key to a vibrant and more influential [ESDI] within NATO."

3. "Failure of the European allies . . . to achieve [DCI] goals would weaken support for the Alliance in the United States."

4. The allies should be pressed "to commit the resources necessary to upgrade their capabilities to rapidly deploy forces over long distances, sustain operations for extended periods of time, and operate jointly with the United States in high-intensity conflicts"—implying, of course, possible allied military actions beyond Europe.

5. Non-EU NATO members should "not be discriminated against, but [should] be fully involved when the European Union addresses issues affecting their security interests."

6. The EU should not "promote a strategic perspective on transatlantic security issues that conflicts with that promoted by [NATO]."

7. There should be no "unnecessary duplication of the resources and capabilities provided by NATO."

---

[1]H. Res. 59, adopted November 2, 1999.

8. Implementing Cologne "should not promote a decline in the military resources that European allies contribute to NATO."[2]

This vigorous catalogue of ministrations about what ESDI/ESDP should and should not do was relieved only by the fact that the resolution passed unanimously—an indication in Senate practice that concerns were not so widely shared as to provoke a debate followed by a formal recorded vote. Nevertheless, coming from a body that only the year before had, in effect, conducted a referendum on continued U.S. commitment to European security by voting (80 to 19) to admit three new members to NATO, this was a clear message to the European allies that they had better tread carefully in developing ESDI: Whether based on valid analysis or at least in part on misunderstanding, widespread displeasure on Capitol Hill was not something to incur lightly.

---

[2]S. Res. 208, adopted November 8, 1999.

Chapter Ten

THE HELSINKI WATERSHED

The "moment of truth" came at the Helsinki EU summit in December 1999. There were a major step forward in ESDP institution building and the resolution, or at least so it seemed at the time, of at least one of the most critical elements of dispute with NATO—i.e., in essence with the United States: the ongoing disagreement about the concept of "NATO first" (although the term was understandably not used in the Helsinki documents).

At Helsinki, the Finnish EU presidency moved forward the work set in motion at Cologne. In a lengthy *Presidency Report*, it proposed for adoption a wide range of provisions for European security and defense and for "non-military crisis management of the European Union"—an area that attracted less attention at the time, but that has subsequently come to have major significance for NATO-EU relations, with a potential import greater than some of the other issues that have been in play between the two institutions.[1]

The most important innovation at Helsinki, following a proposal by Prime Minister Blair and President Chirac,[2] was the setting of a "Headline Goal" to create, by 2003, a capacity to deploy and sustain forces able to pursue the full range of Petersberg Tasks, "including

---

[1] Helsinki European Council, *Presidency Conclusions*, December 10–11 1999, op. cit., especially Annex IV, including Annex 1 to Annex IV, "Presidency Progress Report to the Helsinki European Council on Strengthening the Common European Policy on Security and Defense"; and Annex 2 to Annex IV, "Presidency Report on Non-Military Crisis Management of the European Union."

[2] See Tom Buerkle, "EU Force No Threat to NATO, Allies Say," *International Herald Tribune*, November 26, 1999, p. 1.

the most demanding, in operations up to corps level (up to 15 brigades or 50,000–60,000 persons)"—with provisions for support and rotation, in excess of 200,000 persons all told.[3] The force should be "militarily self-sustaining and have all command and support services needed; it should be deployable within 60 days and be sustainable for at least a year."[4] To make this Headline Goal Task Force possible, the EU decided to create a wide range of command, control, intelligence, and strategic transport capabilities—notably, those areas that, under the 1996 Berlin agreement, would come principally from the United States in the event of a transfer of "NATO

---

[3]This "Headline Goal" was in response to a mandate given to the Finnish EU presidency at the June 1999 European Council summit in Cologne. See Cologne European Council, *Presidency Conclusions,* June 3–4, 1999, op. cit. There has been debate for some time about what the upper limits of the Petersberg Tasks would be. France has tended to be the most ambitious. Thus, in the words of the French ambassador to Washington:

> [W]e are not just aiming at operations on the low end of the peace-keeping spectrum as I have sometimes heard. Does this mean that we would be able, in 2003, to carry out an operation such as "Allied Force" [NATO's Kosovo campaign] entirely by ourselves? Of course not—and it would be dangerous to create such expectations. But the imbalance between U.S. and European forces which we witnessed last year [in the Kosovo conflict] would be substantially reduced—and 2003 will be an important stepping stone on the path to such a capability, which we need to keep as a longer-term goal in order *to be prepared for all non-article 5 contingencies* [emphasis added] (Ambassador François Bujon de l'Estang, Center for Strategic and International Studies, Washington, D.C., October 10, 2000).

[4]Helsinki European Council, *Presidency Conclusions,* December 10–11, 1999, op. cit., Annex 1 to Annex IV:

> To develop European capabilities, Member States have set themselves the headline goal: by the year 2003, cooperating together voluntarily, they will be able to deploy rapidly and then sustain forces capable of the full range of Petersberg Tasks as set out in the Amsterdam Treaty, including the most demanding, in operations up to corps level (up to 15 brigades or 50,000-60,000 persons). These forces should be militarily self-sustaining with the necessary command, control and intelligence capabilities, logistics, other combat support services and additionally, as appropriate, air and naval elements. Member States should be able to deploy in full at this level within 60 days, and within this to provide smaller rapid response elements available and deployable at very high readiness. They must be able to sustain such a deployment for at least one year. This will require an additional pool of deployable units (and supporting elements) at lower readiness to provide replacements for the initial forces.

assets."[5] Furthermore, the European Council adopted measures "relevant to Union involvement in all phases and aspects of crisis management"; decided to engage EU defense ministers, when appropriate, in meetings of the EU's General Affairs Council; and created a number of new permanent political and military bodies within the council:

- A standing Political and Security Committee in Brussels, including national representatives at senior/ambassadorial level.

- The military committee of chiefs of defense, represented by military delegates.

- The military staff to "provide military expertise and support" to what was now renamed the "Common" European Security and Defense Policy (CESDP).[6]

---

[5]Ibid.:

> Member States have also decided to develop rapidly collective capability goals in the fields of command and control, intelligence and strategic transport, areas also identified by the WEU audit. They welcome in this respect decisions already announced by certain Member States which go in that direction:
>
> > to develop and coordinate monitoring and early warning military means;
> >
> > to open existing joint national headquarters to officers coming from other Member States;
> >
> > to reinforce the rapid reaction capabilities of existing European multinational forces;
> >
> > to prepare the establishment of a European air transport command;
> >
> > to increase the number of readily deployable troops;
> >
> > to enhance strategic sea lift capacity.

[6]Ibid.:

> The following new permanent political and military bodies will be established within the Council:
>
> a)—A standing Political and Security Committee (PSC) in Brussels will be composed of national representatives of senior/ambassadorial level. The PSC will deal with all aspects of the CFSP, including the CESDP, in accordance with the provisions of the EU Treaty and without prejudice to

Furthermore, the European Union had already decided at Cologne to create a new post of high representative for the Common Foreign and Security Policy, also with a second title as secretary general of the European Council[7]—thus firmly embedding these critical issues in the EU institution based on the member states rather than in the supranational commission; and to these the Europeans added a third title for this official: secretary general of the Western European Union, as a step on the way toward the WEU's being absorbed within the EU, as envisioned by the Amsterdam Treaty (subject to European Council decision).[8] The appointment of Spain's Javier Solana to all

---

Community competence. In the case of a military crisis management operation, the PSC will exercise, under the authority of the Council, the political control and strategic direction of the operation. For that purpose, appropriate procedures will be adopted in order to allow effective and urgent decision taking. The PSC will also forward guidelines to the Military Committee.

b)—The Military Committee (MC) will be composed of the Chiefs of Defence, represented by their military delegates. The MC will meet at the level of the Chiefs of Defence as and when necessary. This committee will give military advice and make recommendations to the PSC, as well as provide military direction to the Military Staff. The Chairman of the MC will attend meetings of the Council when decisions with defence implications are to be taken.

c)—The Military Staff (MS) within the Council structures will provide military expertise and support to the CESDP, including the conduct of EU-led military crisis management operations. The Military Staff will perform early warning, situation assessment and strategic planning for Petersberg Tasks including identification of European national and multinational forces.

In the meantime, a series of interim bodies were to be set up by March 2000.

[7]See Cologne European Council, *Presidency Conclusions,* June 3–4, 1999, op. cit., "Paragraph II. Staffing Decisions." This second title was conferred in part to ensure that the high representative would be embraced by the bureaucracy of the European Council and would also understand—in part because of his day-to-day duties—that his heart had to lie with the nation-state members of the EU rather than with the EU's supranational expression, as represented by the commission. Comments of a senior EU official to the author, May 2001.

[8]See "Statement by the Secretary General of WEU, Mr. José Cutileiro, on the decision to appoint Dr Javier Solana as the next Secretary General of WEU," Brussels, November 19, 1999; and WEU Ministerial Council, *Luxembourg Declaration,* November 23, 1999:

Ministers . . . expressed their conviction that Mr. Solana's appointment to this position will contribute to the development of relations between WEU and the European Union foreseen in the Treaty on European Union and by the decisions of the European Council in Cologne.

three positions was significant, since he had been serving, until assuming his new duties (October 1999), as NATO's secretary general and thus was able to bring knowledge of its principles and practices to his new work; his appointment also symbolically indicated that the EU's new ventures in foreign policy and defense should not be read as its simply going off in a totally different direction from NATO's.

This leap forward in EU efforts to create a functioning ESDP naturally increased the intensity of U.S. concerns about key elements of the relationship with NATO. The new elements—Political and Security Committee, Military Committee, Military Staff, and secretary general—seemed at first blush to be suspiciously similar to NATO's institutional structure, instantly raising the question whether the EU effort would perforce become a rival for NATO—if only at the bureaucratic level, in terms of time, attention, focus, and overlap, if not also for competition of resources. Could there be—down the road—the prospect of the creation of a second Europe-based "integrated military command structure?" Even though there was hardly a hint at Helsinki of such a development, it was not an unnatural inference that this new institution might develop in such a way.

Much attention was paid to the Headline Goal Task Force (which quickly gained the popular name "rapid reaction force"). But from NATO's standpoint, the most important fact should have been its modesty: the goal of up to 60,000 people could not be seen as producing a competitor for NATO at any serious military task—even factoring in the added support elements and forces that would have to be available for rotation over a deployment period of up to a year. The European rapid reaction force could not, for instance, hope to undertake an operation of the complexity of NATO's efforts during the Kosovo conflict, even if European countries were prepared to emphasize ground operations, with a likely significant exposure to casualties—certainly far higher than would be incurred through an

---

At Cologne, the EU had called for "definition of the modalities for the inclusion of those functions of the WEU which will be necessary for the EU to fulfill its new responsibilities in the area of the Petersberg tasks." The European Council envisioned decisions by the end of 2000, so that "the WEU as an organisation would have completed its purpose" (Cologne European Council, *Presidency Conclusions*, June 3–4, 1999, op. cit., Annex III, paragraph 5).

airpower-only campaign. Some American observers have pointed to the phrase—and similar phrases used later—that the European rapid reaction force would be able to undertake Petersberg Tasks "including the most demanding"; but analyzing the list of those tasks still does not take one into the realm of major military operations.

Another issue was also immediately reintroduced: If the Europeans were engaged in an operation with such complex institutional arrangements, how easily and effectively could they "hand over" operations to NATO if military escalation required that the more capable and robust military organization take over, whether or not that was because some ally came under attack and thus NATO would be charged to respond under the Washington Treaty's Article 5? In effect, would the creation of the European rapid reaction force cross the forbidden line of creating "two NATOs"—although one of them would be "outside" NATO?

But even before these issues were addressed, the United States placed its main focus on what the Helsinki European Council would do to resolve the dispute that had arisen over the differences between the Washington (NATO) and Cologne (EU) texts. The result was hard-won and owed much to pressure from London to ensure that the major Helsinki initiatives did not simply provoke further American disquiet. Thus, the Finnish *Presidency Report* and *Presidency Conclusions* were heavy on important NATO concerns: These included the commitment to develop modalities

> for full consultation, cooperation and transparency between the EU and NATO . . . [and for] necessary dialogue, consultation and cooperation with NATO and its non-EU members. [And the EU states agreed to define] appropriate arrangements [that would] allow . . . non-EU European NATO members and other interested States to contribute to EU military crisis management.[9]

This last point was clearly an effort to deal with some of the expressed concerns of countries like Turkey that wanted to know the extent to which they would be both consulted and engaged.

---

[9]Helsinki European Council, *Presidency Conclusions*, December 10–11, 1999, op. cit., paragraph II: "Common European Policy on Security and Defence."

Despite the bows taken in the right direction, in these instances Helsinki fell short of U.S. hopes. Thus, the "dialogue, consultation and cooperation," noted above, would be done "with full respect for the decision-making autonomy of the EU."[10] Similarly, the EU did decide that "the non-EU European NATO members," after "a decision by the Council to launch an operation," could "participate if they so wish"; and states that were willing to deploy "significant military forces" in an EU-led operation would have "the same rights and obligations as the EU participating Member States in the day-to-day conduct of such an operation." But here, too, the EU offer was qualified. The right of participation by non-EU European NATO members would apply only "in the event of an operation requiring recourse to NATO assets and capabilities." But, "in operations where the EU does not use NATO assets," these countries would have to be invited "on a decision by the Council." Also, terminating an operation would be the council's sole decision.[11]

However, the key, immediate U.S. concern was adequately addressed:

> The European Council underlines its determination to develop an autonomous capacity to take decisions and, *where NATO as a whole is not engaged*, to launch and conduct EU-led military operations in response to international crises. This process will avoid unnecessary duplication and *does not imply the creation of a European army* [emphasis added in both instances].[12]

Since Helsinki, much debate across the Atlantic has turned on whether all the Europeans do subscribe to the principle of "where NATO as a whole is not engaged." For American tastes, it cannot be repeated often enough.[13]

---

[10]Helsinki European Council, *Presidency Conclusions*, December 10–11, 1999, op. cit., Annex 1 to Annex IV, "Consultation and Cooperation with Non-EU Countries and with NATO."

[11]Ibid., Annex 1 to Annex IV.

[12]Ibid., paragraph II. To pin down the point, the key qualifier "where NATO as a whole is not engaged" was repeated twice more in the document.

[13]Some French commentators have sought to modify this phrase by arguing that "where" does not refer to a circumstance—i.e., a choice by NATO—but rather to a place: only "where," in terms of geography, NATO has not already become engaged.

While the logic is not clear, the political import is. Comments made by an EU official in Brussels to the author, May 2001. Obviously, this effort to twist the English language has not had many adherents.

Chapter Eleven

AFTER HELSINKI: GETTING THE NATO-EU RELATIONSHIP RIGHT

Because the Helsinki decisions gave much greater substance and reality to the prospect that a European Security and Defense Policy—and rapid reaction force—could actually come into being, attention began to focus on the precise qualities of the relationship to be forged between NATO and EU/ESDP. Three reasons have already been cited: The risks (however slight) that (1) some sort of competitor for (or even just distraction from) the NATO integrated military command structure could be developing; (2) so much effort would be put into creating ESDP structures that the necessary political will and resources would not be put into building up European defense capabilities, well and truly interoperable within NATO; and (3) the qualifier "unnecessary" of the word "duplication" might be lost sight of as the Europeans sought to create structures that would focus on capacities that would not in fact add to the sum of allied military strength.

Five other factors affecting relations between NATO and EU/ESDP—and thus of concern to the United States about the latter's evolution—either came into play after Helsinki or were intensified by decisions made there. These factors involved (1) military and economic cultures, (2) arm's-length NATO-EU relations, (3) a European caucus in NATO, (4) defense production and trade, and (5) crisis management.

MILITARY AND ECONOMIC CULTURES

One such factor was the progressive diminution of a role for the Western European Union (although it will continue formally to exist for residual Brussels Treaty purposes).[1] For years if not decades, the WEU had served as a form of "buffer" between NATO and the European communities/European Union. Issues arising in the latter body that related to defense questions would, in the main, be shifted over to the sister European organization, if not just dealt with at NATO. At the same time, the WEU was able to bring to bear for NATO some of the perspective of the EU on particular issues—a service that was especially important because of the nature of the career foreign services in Western Europe and the bureaucratic culture of the EU itself. For virtually all these foreign services, to a degree exceeding that in the United States, officers have classically developed a career pattern that is either *political-economic* (and thus, in the realm of European integration, producing assignments and perspectives dealing with EU issues and EU institutions) or that is *political-military* (with a corresponding emphasis on such issues and, institutionally, on the WEU and NATO).[2] Buffer relationships will progressively disappear. Political-military diplomats and other officials will need to be accommodated within EU institutions (and learn to compete within its bureaucracy and with its nonmilitary issues, including competition for resources). In addition, NATO is finding itself creating a relationship with a bureaucracy that, at least at first, seems strange—as opposed to dealing with the WEU.

---

[1]At the Marseille ministerial meeting in November 2000, the European Council also decided "to close down the WEU as an operational body. A smaller, residual structure to service the Modified Brussels Treaty will be established by June 2001." *Foreign and Commonwealth News, European Security and Defence Policy,* December 2000, www. fco.gov.uk/news/keythemepage.asp?PageId=168. See WEU Ministerial Council, *Marseille Declaration,* November 13, 2000.

[2]During the author's service of four and a half years as U.S. ambassador to NATO, only one of his European counterparts had ever served as an ambassador to the European Union, and few had ever served there in any capacity; but most of them from countries belonging to the WEU were "double hatted" to it. A similar pattern applied to more-junior officers, although it has been changing in recent years, with some more "cross-cultural" experiences between economic and military issues.

ARM'S-LENGTH NATO-EU RELATIONS

Another new factor was the added sense of complexity introduced into NATO's dealing with the new EU bodies that were being created. At the best of times, these two institutions have kept one another at arm's length, for a variety of reasons. Significantly, some European states (notably France) have not wanted to risk that NATO (meaning the United States) would unduly influence EU policy and decisions, while others (notably Britain) have at times worried that institutionalizing direct NATO-EU relations would risk giving too much of a role to the supranational European Commission at the expense of the member-state European Council.[3] Thus, NATO and the EU have done surprisingly little to coordinate their respective policies in many critical areas: On the post–cold war agenda they share, these have included engagement in Central Europe, their respective processes for admitting new members, relations with Russia, and involvement in the Balkans—although post-war efforts in both Bosnia and Kosovo have led to progressively better EU-NATO relations in the region, as a matter of necessity.[4] After Helsinki, however, it has become essential that the two institutions cooperate and coordinate with one another, at least on a key range of issues. One result of this pressure—and of this opportunity—has been the joint Solana-Robertson diplomacy on Macedonia in 2001.

This NATO-EU cooperation has acquired particular importance with regard to military planning. Following Berlin in 1996, NATO offered to assume responsibility for conducting the operational planning of WEU military activities, and it did so by working with different notional scenarios provided by the WEU, based on the Petersberg Tasks.[5] But since some European countries, notably France, began to press for the EU's ESDP to have an "autonomous" capability, the

---

[3]While U.S. ambassador, the author, as part of his efforts at NATO to break down some of these barriers and old habits, used to refer to NATO and the EU as "two institutions in the same city living on different planets."

[4]Following the creation of the NATO-led Implementation Force in Bosnia, the author arranged for the first briefings to take place at the North Atlantic Council by Carl Bildt, the high representative (in effect the EU representative) of the Peace Implementation Conference. Not all the Europeans welcomed this interaction.

[5]See footnote 10 of Chapter Three and Chapter Six under the heading "Discriminating," with regard to the NATO role in WEU planning after Berlin 1996.

creation of a separate planning capacity was placed high on the list of priorities. For NATO—and particularly for the United States—this seemed to pose a risk of confusion, especially with the perceived need to create as "seamless" a connection as possible between what military operations the EU might undertake under ESDP—all the more so following the creation of the rapid reaction force—and the potential engagement of NATO if military threat or action escalated to the point where it would have to become engaged. By the same token, NATO would need to know what the EU, through ESDP, was contemplating in terms of operations, in order to assess what military assets might not be available to NATO, even though nominally subject to recall—given that the Europeans' national "NATO" forces and "rapid reaction forces" are, for the most part, one and the same. This NATO need for foreknowledge could exist even in some circumstances "where NATO as a whole were not engaged," but at a time when it could face a challenge elsewhere that would affect military deployments or even operations. This issue of coherence in planning by the two institutions has continued to pose questions; at the very least, it has led NATO to insist on a high degree of transparency in what the EU, through ESDP, is doing or contemplating doing.

EUROPEAN CAUCUS IN NATO

The development of ESDP institutions also raised profound issues about how the EU would make its decisions. Some of these issues have been introduced above, especially the manner in which non-EU NATO members would be able to take part in ESDP military operations—if any were, indeed, ever undertaken; and, as noted earlier, the European Union has been clear about reserving to itself a monopoly of actual decisions about such operations, however much others might be able to take part in the stages, either before these decisions (planning) or afterward (implementation). At the same time, however, the evolution of ESDP and its companion, CFSP, begins to raise in practice an issue that heretofore had only existed in theory—how EU member states would make decisions and then act upon them, within international institutions to which they belong. Most germane to EU/ESDP–NATO relations: Would EU member states seek to act, in effect, as a single unit within NATO bodies, and particularly its premier policymaking organ, the North Atlantic Council?

There is no simple answer. To begin with, as early as the Maastricht Treaty of 1992, the EU had agreed that, following decisions reached by the European Council in the context of CFSP, EU representatives in "international organizations shall cooperate in ensuring that the common positions and common measures adopted by the Council are complied with and implemented."[6] This provision was modified somewhat by the Treaty of Amsterdam (1997), but it still retained its force: "Member States shall coordinate their action in international organisations and at international conferences. They shall uphold the common positions in such fora."[7]

Yet this "theoretical" provision, if implemented, could have major practical effects for the conduct of NATO affairs and especially deliberations within the North Atlantic Council.[8] The council always operates on the principle of consensus and never takes a vote, formal or informal. As a matter of practice, this devotion to consensus is based on twin understandings that no allied country is prepared to cede to others the right to determine circumstances in which its military forces are put at risk and that, when a consensus is indeed reached, NATO honors its commitments—a core quality of the alliance. Classically, the process of reaching consensus has been a matter of give and take among member states, to a remarkable degree actually taking place within the council chamber, as opposed to nations' either bargaining out positions bilaterally between national capitals or simply bringing settled national positions to the council table. Even allies with a greater degree of influence—the United States, first, as well as some of the larger European states—often find themselves influenced decisively by arguments made and ideas advanced by other allies; and what emerges from council discussion are workable compromises that at times actually reflect the preferences of no single ally and not all of what any ally wanted to begin with. Each NATO ambassador—sometimes all of them, including the U.S. ambassador—then undertakes to convince his home government that the

---

[6]See *The Single European Act of 1992*, op. cit., Title V, Article J.6.

[7]See *Consolidated Version of the Treaty on European Union*, op. cit., Title V, Article 19, 1.

[8]From some discussions that took place in late 2000, U.S. diplomats believed they detected efforts at NATO, led by France, to enforce discipline among EU countries. Comments made to the author, December 2000.

(provisionally) agreed course is the best overall, especially because it can gain the precious strength conferred by consensus.[9] Nor has this proved to be a "least common denominator" process, partly because of leadership, especially by the United States, but partly because of the regularity of this method of discussion and agreement, followed for more than half a century, and the seriousness of the stakes for the alliance and its credibility.

To be sure, different groups of allies will talk beforehand about their positions, and on particular issues there can be considerable agreement of views.[10] But to develop what is termed a "European caucus" within NATO would radically change the way in which the North Atlantic Council works. If there were simply an informal comparing of notes and sharing of preferences among the EU states belonging to NATO, that would be one thing; but if the Maastricht/Amsterdam strictures were followed faithfully, then the council could be confronted with a bloc of representatives, each saying more-or-less the same thing, and all unable to vary their national positions without constant consultations—and very likely formal convocation—at the EU in another part of Brussels. Furthermore, in the absence of an acknowledged leader—as the United States is at NATO; in the presence of some EU countries that are not also members of NATO;[11] and with the EU's penchant for "log-rolling" rather than for decisive action, at least not rapid decisive action—such EU-only deliberations are likely to prove least-common-

---

[9]Indeed, the North Atlantic Council has what it calls a "silence procedure," under which a "decision sheet" is agreed upon by the ambassadors, subject to confirmation by all allied governments. A period of "silence" is decreed—perhaps 24–48 hours; if, at the end of that period, no government has "broken silence" (in French, *rompre la silence*), then the provisional decision goes into effect. This method is followed to put pressure on one or more not-quite-convinced governments to go along with the rest of the allies. Even the United States at times finds itself under pressure not to be the nation "breaking silence."

[10]These informal discussions among groups of allies take place in different forums, both at NATO and elsewhere, including bilaterally, with common approaches worked out beforehand. Most notably, these have historically engaged the four largest powers in the alliance: the United States, the U.K., France, and Germany.

[11]The "back-door" involvement of non-NATO EU members in the NATO decision process, even indirectly, would be at variance with an unspoken NATO principle that the countries making the decisions should be those that would have to incur (share) any ensuing risks.

denominator.[12] For the United States, in particular—although also for other non-EU NATO members—this challenge to the North Atlantic Council's capacity to function effectively would be too high a price to pay for honoring a particular aspect in the development of an ESDP that may not in fact undertake serious security responsibilities, at least in areas and in circumstances where NATO might consider becoming engaged. Indeed, this issue is one of the few in the NATO-ESDP debate both on which the United States has taken a strong position and to which the Europeans should pay careful heed.

DEFENSE PRODUCTION AND TRADE

As ESDP became more serious, five principal issues came to the fore in regard to European defense industries. First, it had been clear since the early post–cold war period that allied defense budgets would fall—as indeed they have done—and thus there would be less work for existing European defense industries. Among other things, economic reality began to press for consolidation of companies and of whole sectors of the European defense industry, including across national boundaries, with the sharing of critical activities like research and development and with other economies of scale. As so often happens, politicians were slower to respond than industry, but by the late 1990s, consolidation fever from the United States had finally spread to Europe. This was a contagion, incidentally, that U.S. defense companies had themselves urged the Europeans to "catch," so that there would be both viable European partners (where this was both possible and sensible in business terms) and the likelihood of a continuing European military market.[13]

Second, as ESDP began to enter the realm of potentially (1) enabling the EU to take military action, through commitment to create a rapid reaction force, and (2) considering capabilities needed to make this or any other capacity a reality, the Europeans began to place added

---

[12]It is most doubtful that, if the EU had had a "European caucus" at NATO in 1995, the alliance would have decided to use airpower in defense of Bosnian safe areas. The case is less clear-cut in regard to NATO's Kosovo operations in 1999, but the point is still instructive.

[13]See, for instance, Vance D. Coffman, Chairman and CEO, Lockheed Martin Corporation, *Bridges Are Better Than Walls,* the Lockheed Martin Paris Air Show Press Dinner, Ritz Hotel, Paris, June 17, 2001.

emphasis on the means of producing defense goods and especially the potential for cooperation among the ESDP countries and companies. This emphasis has extended to the point that some ESDP countries have put pressure on non-EU countries to "buy European," as opposed to U.S. defense products.[14]

Third, pressures from the United States both to keep European defense spending from falling and to embark on the ambitious Defense Capabilities Initiative necessarily increased interest in Europe about the role of indigenous defense industries. In short, if the allies were to be expected to increase their contribution to the common military effort, then European companies, along with European workers and the technological base, should share in the benefits. In addition, if the United States were concerned about an increase in the European part of burden sharing, then there should be an increase in the Europeans' capacity to produce defense goods, especially at the high end of technology, which is most critical to sustain interoperability, rather than having to secure these goods from the United States.

Fourth, European leaders were alert to the industrial aspects of European integration as it played out within the military realm. Indeed, this theme was routinely included in presentations about the future of ESDP. Thus at the Cologne EU summit, the leaders

> recognize[d] the need to undertake sustained efforts to strengthen the industrial and technological defence base, which we want to be competitive and dynamic. . . . [They were] determined to foster the restructuring of the European defence industries . . . [and would] . . . work towards closer and more efficient defence industry collaboration. We will seek further progress in the harmonisation of military requirements and the planning and procurement of arms.[15]

Indeed, "enhanced cooperation in the field of armaments with the aim of creating a European armament agency" had been a goal as

---

[14]Poland, for example, has been pressed by some EU states to buy European as opposed to U.S. defense goods. The argument made is that "the U.S. got you into NATO, but only we can get you into the EU." Comments made to the author by Polish officials, February 2001. Pressures on Norway were discussed above.

[15]See Cologne European Council, *Presidency Conclusions,* June 3–4, 1999, op. cit., "Annex III," paragraph 2.

early as the Maastricht Treaty of 1992.[16] Similar statements have been made at subsequent European Council summits;[17] and the Nice summit (December 2000) identified a number of

> vital projects which would contribute to bolstering the capabilities at the Union's disposal: The Future Large Aircraft (Airbus A400M), maritime transport vessels, Troop Transport Helicopters (MH 90).[18]

Not surprisingly, these projects focused on force mobility, as foreshadowed by the move to create the European rapid reaction force. Whether these projects reflect "unnecessary duplication" from the U.S. point of view has been discussed earlier: But the bottom-line issue could be whether the Europeans would otherwise be spending such moneys on defense at all.

It was also during this period that major steps were taken regarding the consolidation of European defense industries: notable were the acquisition by British Aerospace (BAe) of the defense electronics division of GEC-Marconi (announced January 1999) and, in part as a response to that unexpected step, the creation of the European Aeronautic Defense and Space Company—a merger of Aerospatiale Matra S.A. (France), Construcciones AeronNáuticas S.A. (Spain), and DaimlerChrysler Aerospace AG (Germany), which became a publicly traded company in July 2000. These and other steps followed the conclusion of a letter of intent signed by the defense ministers of Britain, France, Germany, Italy, Spain, and Sweden in July 1998 to promote formal arrangements among defense companies across national boundaries, "to facilitate the restructuring of the European

---

[16]See *Treaty on European Union;* February 7, 1992, op. cit.; and the treaty's "Final Act: Declaration on Western European Union," paragraph B.4.

[17]Thus at Helsinki, the *Presidency Conclusions* noted that

> Member States welcome the recent progress made towards the restructuring of European defense industries, which constitutes an important step forward. This contributes to strengthening the European industrial and technological defence base. Such developments call for increased efforts to seek further progress in the harmonisation of military requirements and the planning and procurement of arms, as Member States consider appropriate (Helsinki European Council, December 10–11, 1999, op. cit.).

[18]See Nice European Council, *Presidency Report on the European Security and Defense Policy,* December 7–9, 2000, paragraph 5.

defence industry."[19] Furthermore, as early as November 1996, France, Germany, the U.K., and Italy had "started a global process to manage their armament programmes jointly." This led to creation of the Joint Armaments Cooperation Organisation (OCCAR), which formally gained legal status in September 1998.[20] At the time, UK Defence Minister George Robertson said:

> An increasing proportion of the United Kingdom's equipment requirements are likely to be met by collaborative projects in future, and OCCAR was created with the specific aim of improving the way these projects are managed.[21]

---

[19]See *Letter of Intent Between 6 Defence Ministers on Measures to Facilitate the Restructuring of the European Defence Industry*, London, July 6, 1998 (http://projects. sipri.se/expcon/loi/lointent.htm). Another significant combination was the acquisition by Thomson-CSF of the UK firm Racale in January 2000; the company is now known as Thales.

[20]*Organisme Conjoint de Coopération en matière d'Armement* (OCCAR) has four principles:

> Creation of transnational integrated program teams, and the use of modern, high-performance methods to manage the programs;
>
> Consolidation and development of the European industrial and technological defense base;
>
> Application of a global "juste retour" principle over several programs and several years;
>
> Preference, in procurement decisions, for materials developed with the participation of countries belonging to OCCAR, their participation being within the context of the organization (*The French Armaments Policy: Institutional Framework for Cooperation: OCCAR*, www.defense.gouv.fr/actualites/dossier/d26e/fiche2.html).

Also speech by Alain Richard, May 17, 2001, op. cit. Richard argued that, by 2001, OCCAR was "now gaining more influence," noting that it "has already integrated its first program and gained a legal status last January. This is a precious tool for the development of a coherent armament policy on a European basis." He foresaw other countries joining. Ibid. In addition, the Europeans have had the Western European Armaments Group. See, for instance, WEU Ministerial Council, *Marseille Declaration*, November 13, 2000.

[21]*Defence Systems Daily: Farnborough 98 News*, "European Defence Ministers Sign OCCAR Treaty," September 10, 1998. However, later that year, a House of Commons Select Committee of Defence, in approving the OCCAR Convention, noted that

> There remains . . . a disappointing lack of agreement amongst the governments of its member states about OCCAR's place in European defence in the

As French Minister of Defense Alain Richard put the point in May 2001:

> The complexity of technology and the high level of fixed costs is [sic] a strong incentive for us [Europeans] to join our forces and share the effort. The only way for our companies and research agencies to achieve the highest standards, is to combine our assets and capabilities.[22]

But what effects will these steps toward consolidation—and potentially cost savings—of European defense companies have on European capabilities and relations with counterparts across the Atlantic? Neither part of the question can yet be answered with any certainty. In theory, consolidation and rationalization should provide the Europeans with "greater bang for the Euro," but whether this will also lead to effective pressure to reduce defense ties across the Atlantic is more problematic—a side effect of the development of ESDP. This reduction is not foreordained; indeed, there has been a thickening of company-to-company relationships across the Atlantic, including some European purchases of U.S. firms and even acceptance by the U.S. Defense Department of European participation in some major U.S. defense projects—notably the Joint Strike Fighter, highlighted by the significant role for BAe in Lockheed Martin's successful bid.[23]

Fifth, defense industry relationships across the Atlantic are deeply affected by one development that would have existed even if there were no ESDP, but that is more important because of the ESDP's creation: the sharing of U.S. military high technology with European partners. Given that most (though certainly not all) such advances

---

longer term, and about OCCAR's relationship with the North Atlantic Alliance. Unless that vision begins to emerge soon, there is a risk that OCCAR, like so many of its predecessors have done, will begin to lose its way (*House of Commons Select Committee of Defence Approves OCCAR Convention,* UK House of Commons, December 6, 1998, www.parliament. uk/commons/selcom90/defpnt2.htm).

[22]He saw this as "especially true for the UK and France, which concentrate together more than two thirds of the overall defense R&D in the whole of Europe" (speech by Alain Richard, May 17, 2001, op. cit.).

[23]BAe has become the fifth-largest supplier of defense goods to the Pentagon, chiefly through U.S.-owned subsidiaries.

take place in the United States, clearly the effort to preserve the capacity for interoperability among allied forces requires broad access to the same or similar technologies—although, in some areas, what is called "open architecture" can permit a European military to make use of American capabilities without having access to the so-called black box of the most sensitive technology. But this is an imperfect solution, one that is not politically acceptable over the long term for many if not most European governments, and also one that is likely to stimulate an increase in European efforts to have the potential for developing military capacities independent of the United States.

Furthermore, if the United States presses European allies to join in coalition operations beyond Europe—either as formal NATO operations or as "coalitions of the able and willing"—then issues of interoperability gain in importance. If the United States wants allied cooperation in such operations, it will have to be more responsive with the sharing of defense high technology.[24] Given that the political culture in the United States since the end of the cold war has been to focus on coalition operations, as a matter of risk sharing, U.S. domestic politics, and maximizing international support, this is a highly significant point.

The United States has been slow to respond to European concerns about the sharing of U.S. high technology in the defense field, although it has taken some steps. In February 2000, U.S. Defense Secretary William Cohen and UK Secretary of State for Defence Geoff Hoon signed a declaration of principles that provided special, reciprocal treatment for one another's defense companies (including in the area of classified information), such that "UK defence companies doing business in the US should be treated no less favorably than US

---

[24]Such operations are certainly implied by NATO's Defense Capabilities Initiative. See *Defence Capabilities Initiative*, April 25, 1999, op. cit. :

> The objective of this initiative is to improve defence capabilities to ensure the effectiveness of future multinational operations across the full spectrum of Alliance missions, in the present and foreseeable security environments [paragraph 1]. Potential threats to Alliance security are more likely to result from regional conflicts, ethnic strife or other crises beyond Alliance territory [paragraph 2]. Operations outside Alliance territory may need to be undertaken with no, or only limited, access to existing NATO infrastructure [paragraph 3].

defence companies doing business in the UK."[25] Several other European nations objected to the "exclusive" nature of this arrangement; but it was designed to have broader involvement of other allies.[26] In May 2000, U.S. Secretary of State Albright launched a Defense Trade Security Initiative at the Florence foreign ministers' meeting of the North Atlantic Council.[27] This initiative consisted of some 17 changes to U.S. procedures, including the way in which export licenses would be granted for particular defense products.[28] These are "steps on the way," but they have not resolved all the outstanding problems sufficiently to create a climate of cooperation and to end European concerns.

This issue of the so-called two-way street in defense arrangements continues to pose difficulties for U.S.-European cooperation, including resolution of matters affecting NATO-EU/ESDP relations and attitudes on both sides of the Atlantic about those relations.

CRISIS MANAGEMENT

With the complex arrangements worked out at Helsinki, another aspect of ESDP became more apparent and provided a stark contrast with NATO. Put simply, as part of a broader European CFSP, ESDP is designed to function as an instrument for the former; NATO, by contrast, is much more "stand alone." As a military alliance, although with political-military aspects, NATO has never developed mecha-

---

[25]See American Embassy London Office of Defence Cooperation, February 5, 2000. Secretary of Defense William Cohen said:

> We hope that this will help facilitate even greater interaction between our respective industries so that we can have a harmonized approach to sharing technology, working cooperative and partnership arrangements and potentially mergers as well (Secretary of Defense William Cohen and U.K. Secretary of State for Defence Geoffrey Hoon, *Pentagon News Briefing on Bilateral Defense Cooperation*, February 5, 2000).

[26]Secretary Cohen, ibid.: "We hope to consider other countries, Germany among them. We are pursuing this with several countries."

[27]See Philip T. Reeker, Acting Spokesman, *Defense Trade Security Initiative*, Press Statement, U.S. Department of State, May 24, 2000.

[28]See *Seventeen Agreed Proposals of the Defense Trade Security Initiative,* Fact Sheet, U.S. Department of State, Bureau of Political Military Affairs, Washington, D.C., May 26, 2000.

nisms for conducting a "foreign policy," or even "crisis management." NATO's secretary general (who also serves as chairman of the
North Atlantic Council) is not a foreign minister reporting to a government, with broad latitude to act on behalf of the institution, even
though, on occasion, he has been given a special and limited mandate to negotiate with other governments on behalf of the council,
for example, in conclusion of the NATO-Russia Founding Act in 1997
and in diplomacy over Macedonia (jointly with the EU's Javier
Solana) in 2001. In addition, the NATO secretary general's "mas-
ter"—the council—does not function like an independent government but remains a collection of representatives of sovereign governments. Thus, for neither of NATO's only two sustained uses of
force—Bosnia in 1995 and Kosovo in 1999—did the North Atlantic
Council have a direct role in the diplomacy leading up to, or during,
conflict; at the time of both conflicts, that responsibility rested, at
least formally, with the so-called Contact Group that, while including
some NATO allies, had no connection with the alliance and did not
always keep NATO fully informed of what it was doing.[29] Similarly, in
leading the two peacekeeping forces (SFOR and KFOR), NATO does
not also have overall political responsibility for what happens in its
areas of operation; responsibility is bifurcated.[30] To be sure, at the
April 1999 Washington summit, the allies did agree that

> This new Alliance will be . . . able to undertake new missions
> including contributing to effective conflict prevention and *engaging
> actively in crisis management*, including crisis response operations
> [emphasis added].[31]

The aspiration, however, made no provision for its achievement.

---

[29]NATO planning was available for negotiators at the Dayton peace talks of autumn
1995; by contrast, this was not done for the Rambouillet talks over Kosovo in spring
1999—one reason, it could be argued, for the failure of those negotiations.

[30]The relative success of UN operations in Eastern Slavonia (the United Nations
Transitional Administration in Eastern Slavonia), as opposed to those in Bosnia, is often credited, at least in part, to the fact that political and military responsibility were
unified—for much of the time under the leadership of a U.S. foreign service officer,
Jacques Klein, who also happened to be a major general in the U.S. Air Force Reserve.

[31]NATO, *Washington Summit Communiqué*, April 24, 1999, op. cit., paragraph 2.

By contrast, CFSP and ESDP are designed and constructed to have crisis management responsibilities: indeed, the capacity (in theory) to deal with a situation from start to finish. Thus, the December 1999 Helsinki European Council mandated that

> a non-military crisis management mechanism will be established to coordinate and make more effective the various civilian means and resources, in parallel with the military ones, at the disposal of the Union and the Member States.[32]

This was based on an inventory of member state capacities, which showed they "have accumulated considerable experience or have considerable resources in a number of areas." It was also concluded that the

> Union needs to strengthen the responsiveness and efficiency of its resources and tools . . . [and] to draw up an action plan . . . to develop a rapid reaction capability in the field of crisis management using non-military instruments.[33]

There would be "the development of a military crisis management capability as well as a civilian one."[34] The EU would also have the

---

[32]See Helsinki European Council, *Presidency Conclusions,* December 10–11, 1999, op. cit., paragraph 28. The report mandated carrying work forward "including conflict prevention and a committee for civilian crisis management" (ibid., paragraph 29).

[33]Ibid., Annex 2 to Annex IV, among other things:

The Union should aim at:

— strengthening the synergy and responsiveness of national, collective and NGO resources in order to avoid duplication and improve performance, while maintaining the flexibility of each contributor to decide on the deployment of assets and capabilities in a particular crisis, or via a particular channel;

— enhancing and facilitating the EU's contributions to, and activities within, other organisations, such as the UN and the OSCE whenever one of them is the lead organisation in a particular crisis, as well as EU autonomous actions;

— ensuring inter-pillar coherence.

[34]See Santa Maria da Feira European Council, *Presidency Conclusions,* June 19–20, 2000, paragraph I.C. There was even some thinking that an EU capacity in this area could be made available "to the transatlantic community"—implying NATO, espe-

benefit of a single individual in at least nominal charge: the secretary general of the council and high representative—who is also secretary general of the WEU.[35]

This disparity between the formal competence of CFSP/ESDP (policies of the EU) on the one hand and NATO on the other may never become of material importance—and the tandem ESDP-NATO diplomacy over Macedonia in 2001 offers a hopeful prospect. But in theory, at least, the European arrangements have the advantage, in terms of being able to conduct a crisis management operation that does not require a formal handing over of responsibility from one institution to another—with all of the inherent difficulties that such a process could entail.[36] In contrast to some other ESDP developments, however, this one should not be seen as a challenge to NATO but rather as highlighting the latter's own lack of competence—in the institutional sense of the term—in relation to what are likely to be real-world security situations in the future. The issue is not to try limiting what the EU does through ESDP, or even primarily to make ESDP compatible with NATO's capabilities and methods of operation, as desirable as the latter would be, but rather to find means whereby the alliance—and more particularly the North Atlantic Council, as well as the military commands—can be linked to processes of diplomacy and crisis management that may largely determine what practical responsibilities NATO is called upon to exercise. This 21st-century challenge to NATO and to its relationship to the "pre-military action" world of diplomacy and crisis management would have existed even if ESDP and CFSP had never been invented.

---

cially in circumstances when the United States did not want to be engaged "in the management of a crisis." See Alain Richard, February 3, 2001, op. cit.

[35]In comparing NATO and the EU in terms of crisis-management capability, it must be acknowledged that the EU's institutions will only be able to act where the member states will permit, and that there will continue, at least for some time, to be a relatively "short leash"; but the EU will be able to bring to bear civilian instruments beyond those that NATO can muster or, as discussed later, instruments "such as mine clearance, customs, mediation, training of police or judges" (www.europa.eu.int/comm/external_relations/cfsp/news/ip_01_255.htm).

[36]Diplomacy prior to the Kosovo conflict is a pertinent example of NATO's being brought late into the process of dealing with an emerging crisis.

Chapter Twelve

PRACTICAL ARRANGEMENTS: DEVIL IN THE DETAILS (II)

Following the initiatives taken at Helsinki, by the time of the European Council summit at Santa Maria da Feira (June 19–20, 2000), the EU had made major strides toward developing the modalities of the new ESDP, especially in a variety of areas designed to develop "a military crisis management capability as well as a civilian one."[1] Two efforts, however, stand out: the ESDP's relationship to third parties in Europe (NATO members and aspirants to join the EU) and its relationship directly with NATO.[2] Throughout, the Portuguese *Presidency Report* to the council is careful to reiterate "the decision-making autonomy of the EU."

---

[1]Santa Maria da Feira European Council, *Presidency Conclusions,* June 19–20, 2000, op. cit., paragraph C.6. See also "Annex I, Presidency Report on Strengthening the Common European Security and Defence Policy."

[2]The Santa Maria da Feira European Council *Presidency Report* also dealt with provisions for civilian crisis management, focusing especially on

> acting to prevent the eruption or escalation of conflicts; consolidating peace and internal stability in periods of transition; [and] ensuring complementarity between the military and civilian aspects of crisis management covering the full range of Petersberg tasks. . . . [Furthermore, t]his process could be built outwards step-by-step to cover a wide range of limited as well as complex civil crisis management operations (ibid., "Appendix 3, Study on Concrete Targets on Civilian Aspects of Crisis Management," paragraph A).

Particular attention would be paid to creating a police capability (5,000 officers by 2003) and strengthening the rule of law, civilian administration, and civil protection (ibid., paragraphs B–D and Appendix 4).

Regarding ESDP's relationship to third parties, the EU at Santa Maria da Feira set out a number of formal processes "to identify . . . arrangements for dialogue, consultation and cooperation on issues related to crisis management ensuring the decision-making autonomy of the EU."[3] As a matter of principle, "exchanges with the non-EU European NATO members" would be "when the subject matter requires it, such as on questions concerning the nature and functioning of EU-led operations using NATO assets and capabilities."[4] During the "interim period"—until final arrangements were made, slated to be agreed upon at the Nice summit in December 2000— there would be two meetings during each EU presidency between the EU and the 15 candidates for membership; and also two meetings with the 6 non-EU European NATO members.[5] And for the "permanent phase" of ESDP, there would be EU+15 and EU+6 meetings during any "routine phase"—i.e., when there was no crisis to be considered.[6] During an "operational phase," the non-EU European NATO members could take part when there was "recourse to NATO assets and capabilities," but they would have to be invited by the council to take part "when the EU does not use NATO assets."[7]

> Other countries—candidates for EU admission—may also be invited . . . to take part in EU-led operations. . . . [Every country taking part in an operation,] by deploying significant military forces, will have the same rights and obligations as the EU participating Member States in the day to day conduct of that operation,[8] . . . [although termination of an operation would be done solely by the council, after consultations with those other participating countries].[9]

---

[3]Ibid., paragraph C.

[4]Ibid., "Appendix I, Arrangements to Be Concluded by the Council on Modalities of Consultation and/or Participation That Will Allow the Non-EU European NATO Members and Other Countries Which Are Candidates for Accession to the EU to Contribute to EU Military Crisis Management," paragraph 6.

[5]Ibid., paragraphs 8–12.

[6]Ibid., paragraphs 14–16.

[7]Ibid., paragraph 19.

[8]Ibid., paragraph 20.

[9]Ibid., paragraph 22.

This tightly drawn "lawyer's document" is notable for three features: The EU reserves control over all key elements of ESDP activities; non-EU European NATO members are ensured of participation only if NATO assets are used—thus potentially creating a political fissure among European states, however minor it might be in practical terms in view of the limited likelihood of any significant EU military operation under ESDP; and there is no mention in the document of any consultations with the United States or Canada. That lapse, in itself, was not confidence-inspiring in Washington; the message seemed clear—this effort is about Europeans, not about broader associations with the transatlantic world.

By the same token, according to the agreements at Santa Maria da Feira, EU "consultations and cooperation" with NATO were again premised on "full respect [for] the autonomy of EU decision-making."[10] But there was a useful—and virtually essential—bow to the importance of the Defense Capabilities Initiative: "EU-objectives in the field of military capabilities and those arising, for those countries concerned, from NATO's [DCI], will be mutually reinforcing."[11]

The method chosen here was to propose to NATO four

> ad hoc working groups . . . [on] security issues, capabilities goals, modalities enabling EU access to NATO assets and capabilities and the definition of permanent arrangements for EU-NATO consultation.[12]

They would tackle each of these issues:

- *Security:* The ad hoc working group should reach an agreement, especially regarding "information exchange and access by designated officials from the EU and its Member States to NATO planning structures." This should lead to a EU-NATO security agreement.[13]

---

[10]Santa Maria da Feira European Council, *Presidency Report,* June 19–20, 2000, op. cit., "Annex I, Appendix 2, Principles for Consultation with NATO on Military Issues and Recommendations on Developing Modalities for EU/NATO Relations," paragraph 1.

[11]Ibid., paragraph 2.

[12]Ibid., Annex I, paragraph D.

[13]Ibid., Annex I, Appendix 2, paragraph A.1.; also paragraph B.2(a).

- *Defining capability goals:* The group would devise modalities for the relationship to DCI, cited above, to "permit the EU to draw, as needed, on NATO military expertise." Furthermore—as implicit testament to the practical value EU/ESDP seeks to gain from NATO—

  > Member States would use existing defence planning procedures including, as appropriate, those available in NATO and the Planning and Review Process of the PfP [Partnership for Peace].[14]

- *EU access to NATO assets and capabilities:* The group would focus on two variants: when the EU would use NATO assets and when it would not, with the goal of drawing up an "agreement," to "be ready by the time the EU becomes operational." Notably, the document identifies where the EU thinks the difficulty lies: "The EU looks forward to substantial progress *within NATO* [emphasis added]."[15]

- *Defining permanent arrangements:* The group would work out the nature of EU-NATO relations, "which would formalise structures and procedures for consultation between the two organisations in times of crisis and non-crisis."[16]

Given that these procedures were drafted by the EU, it is not surprising that they are very much focused on what the EU would want and expect from NATO, as well as on the means for the EU's keeping control over its own processes, especially in regard to non-EU NATO members: Good drafting but not necessarily good politics. Except for a ritual bow to the importance of the Defense Capabilities Initiative, there is nothing offered in these modalities to reassure NATO (meaning Washington, in particular), including on issues relating to the avoidance of a bifurcation of security responsibilities between the two institutions, the possibility for NATO's oversight of transferred assets, its right of recall of those assets, the importance of preserving the integrity of NATO's command structure, etc. Indeed,

---

[14]Ibid., paragraph A.2.; also see paragraph B.2(b).

[15]Ibid., paragraph A.3.; also see paragraph B.2(c).

[16]Ibid., paragraph B.2(d). and paragraph A.4.

nowhere in the Feira *Presidency Conclusions* does the stock phrase "where NATO as a whole is not engaged" appear—although it could be argued that this was a "modalities" rather than a "policy" document; nevertheless, much policy lurks in modalities. A process was to begin; but its very presentation did not show the kind of sensitivity that the United States—and some other allies—had been looking for; it had too much of the "Europe-firsters," and not enough leavening by countries on which the United States was relying to protect NATO interests. This illustrates some of the irony of the entire NATO–EU/ESDP process: Since fully 11 of the 15 ESDP members are also members of NATO, it must seem strange that so much of what is drafted by the EU appears as though no NATO-friendly hand had touched it.

Chapter Thirteen

PARALLEL TRACKS

During the latter half of 2000, the EU/ESDP and NATO could be said to be moving on parallel tracks: but as in Euclidean geometry, moving in a similar direction, not converging. The former followed what, in EU terms, is the inexorable logic of implementing decisions already made—i.e., reducing them to bureaucratic practice. These focused on the four working groups set up with NATO, where "WEU-NATO relations have paved the way for the EU's relationship with NATO. And the European Union is now close to defining its proposals on cooperation with NATO";[1] the building up of formal contacts between the two institutions—as they circled one another warily; the EU's seeking to gain the benefits of association with NATO but at minimal compromise of "autonomy"; and especially reaching the moment at which the members of the European Union would make formal commitments of the forces they would provide to a notional Headline Goal Task Force, as it was to be developed in the period to 2003.

The key event took place on November 20, a so-called Capabilities Commitment Conference of EU defense ministers in Brussels—defining for the long term what at NATO would be called "force generation" at a time of preparing for military action. This resulted in creation of a "Force Catalogue," providing for "a pool of more than 100,000 persons and approximately 400 combat aircraft and 100 ves-

---

[1]WEU Secretary General Javier Solana, *WEU Council of Ministers' Session at 21,* Marseille, November 13, 2000.

sels."[2] This catalogue included potential contributions from 14 of the 15 EU states (Denmark did not take part).[3] There were also commitments from 6 other countries, including 4 of the countries aspiring for EU membership (see Table 2). Among other things, this last step was implicit recognition that the EU member states were not, even notionally, making available all the forces that could be needed.[4]

In line with the decisions made at the Helsinki and Feira European Councils, member states at the Capabilities Commitment Confer-

---

[2]See *Military Capabilities Commitment Declaration*, Brussels, November 20, 2000. Notably, the declaration including most of the language that NATO looked for in such documents, including the phrase "where NATO as a whole is not engaged. . . . This process, without unnecessary duplication, does not involve the establishment of a European army" (Ibid., paragraph 1). This last phrase about a "European army" was reportedly put in EU documents at the behest of the Irish, for reasons of its long-standing neutrality. See Brian Cowen, T.D., Irish Minister for Foreign Affairs, "Let's Share in EU's Great Future," *Irish Examiner*, May 14, 2001:

> Another much repeated and equally erroneous claim is that a European Army is being established, with Ireland's participation. The EU Headline Goal, or so-called Rapid Reaction Force, is emphatically not a standing army. . . . The EU's High Representative for [CFSP], Mr Javier Solana, clearly set out the position in a speech in Dublin last year when he said "All member States are agreed that the Union is not in the business of creating a European Army. That is quite clear." And if that is not enough, these facts have been repeatedly recognised by the conclusions of several European Councils, including most recently at Nice.

[3]J.A.C. Lewis, *Jane's Defence*, November 30, 2000, www.janes.com/defence/news/jdw/jdw001130_2_n.shtml:

> The largest contributor to the force will be Germany, which has pledged 13,500 ground troops, while the UK has committed 12,500 and France 12,000. Italy and Spain will each contribute up to 6,000 and the Dutch 5,000. Other contributions range from Greece's 3,500 to Luxembourg's 100. Of the 15 EU nations, only Denmark has declined to take part.

[4]*Military Capabilities Commitment Declaration*, November 20, 2000, op. cit., supplemental paragraph:

> Contributions received at the ministerial meetings on 21 November [with other states] will extend the range of capabilities available for EU-led operations, thus enabling the EU's intervention capability to be strengthened in the manner most appropriate to the circumstances.

Table 2

November 20, 2000, EU Force Catalogue (Extracts)

Nation	Contribution
Germany	13,500 troops, 20 ships, 93 aircraft
France	12,000 troops, 15 ships, Helios observation satellites, 75 aircraft
Spain	6,000 troops, one air-naval group based around an aircraft carrier, 40 aircraft
United Kingdom	12,500 troops, 18 ships, 72 aircraft
Austria	2,000 troops
Sweden	1,500 troops
Greece	3,500 troops
Luxembourg	100 troops
The Netherlands	5,000 troops
Finland	2,000 troops
Ireland	1,000 troops
Italy	6,000 troops
Portugal	1,000 troops
Belgium	1,000 troops, 9 ships, 25 aircraft
Denmark	No contribution by virtue of a derogation from the Amsterdam Treaty in regard to defense
Total	67,100 troops

ence pledged to supply, on a voluntary basis, national contributions to meeting the rapid reaction capability identified for the achievement of the Headline Goal. They announced their initial commitments as indicated in Table 2 and also said that:

> The above figures are provisional. . . . The pool is also likely to be supplemented by contributions from third countries wishing to play their part in an EU-led operation. At the Capabilities Commitment Conference, Turkey informed the Fifteen that it was prepared to offer the future rapid reaction force some 5,000 troops, Norway

pledged 1,200, the Czech Republic roughly 1,000, Hungary 450, Poland 1,000 (Framework Brigade) and Slovakia 350.[5]

But the Capabilities Commitment Conference did not just focus on a potential "wish list" of forces to be available for the European rapid reaction force—forces, of course, that in the main were the same ones that would be committed to NATO operations; it also took account of shortfalls. This was possibly in response, at least in part, to American criticisms. Thus, the conference identified

> a number of areas in which efforts will be made in upgrading existing assets, investment, development and coordination so as gradually to acquire or enhance the capabilities required for autonomous EU action.[6]

And while "analysis" of the Force Catalogue showed that "by 2003" the EU would

> be able to carry out the full range of Petersberg tasks . . . certain capabilities need to be improved both in quantitative and qualitative terms in order to maximise the capabilities available to the Union. . . . To that end, [the member states] will aim to identify as soon as possible the complementary initiatives which they may implement.[7]

This admonition to do better also revealed an ongoing tension between the potential use of NATO assets and gaining the capacity for "autonomy of action."[8] In general, the EU member states "commit-

---

[5]*Building the Means and Capabilities for Crisis Management Under the CESDP,* Reply to the Annual Report of the Council, submitted on behalf of the Defence Committee by Mr. Rapson, Rapporteur, WEU Assembly, Document A/1715 Addendum, December 1, 2000.

[6]Ibid., paragraph 3.

[7]Ibid., paragraph 4.

[8]Thus, regarding

> command, control and communications, the Member States offered a satisfactory number of national or multinational headquarters. . . . These officers will have to be evaluated further . . . so that the EU can, in addition to possible recourse to NATO capabilities, have the best possible command and control resources at its disposal. The Union pointed out the importance it

ted themselves . . . to continue taking steps to strengthen their own capabilities and carrying out existing or planned projects."[9] They also recognized "the need for mutual reinforcement of the EU's capability goals and those arising, for the countries concerned, from the DCI."[10] This was to be part of a broader "evaluation mechanism" with regard to meeting the Headline Goal, while also recognizing that what the EU through ESDP did would have an impact on NATO. Thus, they committed to "take steps to ensure the coherent development of EU

---

attaches to the speedy conclusion of ongoing talks on access to NATO capabilities and assets (ibid., paragraph 4).

Another area where ESDP was very much dependent on NATO, but where independent capability could aid the goal of "autonomy," was satellite imaging:

Some [EU Member States] undertook to improve the Union's *guaranteed access* to satellite imaging, thanks in particular to the development of new optical and radar satellite equipment (Helios II, SAR Lupe and Cosmos Skymed) [emphasis added] (ibid., paragraph 5).

In addition, an "evaluation mechanism" would need to be defined.

In order to avoid unnecessary duplication, it will, for the Member States concerned [e.g., NATO members], rely on technical data emanating from existing NATO mechanisms such as the Defence Planning Process and the Planning and Review Process (PARP). . . . In addition, exchange of information and transparency would be appropriately ensured [between NATO and the EU] . . . to ensure the coherent development of EU and NATO capabilities where they overlap (ibid.).

[9]Ibid., paragraph 5:

These projects as a whole relate to:

- improving the performance of European forces in respect of the availability, deployability, sustainability and interoperability of those forces;

- developing "strategic" capabilities: strategic mobility to deliver the forces rapidly to the field of operations; headquarters to command and control the forces and the associated information and communication system; means of providing the forces with intelligence information;

- strengthening essential operational capabilities in the framework of a crisis-management operation; areas which were identified in this context were: resources for search and rescue in operational conditions, means of defence against ground-to-ground missiles, precision weapons, logistic support, simulation tools.

[10]Ibid., paragraph 6(g).

and NATO capabilities where they overlap," and that arrangements with NATO include "transparency, cooperation and dialogue."[11]

Also important, from the point of view of NATO and U.S. attitudes, the Capabilities Commitment Conference delved into other areas. One stands out. The conference explored the possibility of using command headquarters separate from NATO's, including separate from NATO's Combined Joint Task Force (CJTF) headquarters, which had been offered to WEU in 1996 and which has exercised in a WEU mode since that time.[12] Thus, the conference noted that the member states offer "a satisfactory number of national or multinational headquarters at strategic, operational, force and component levels."[13] Some evaluation of these offers would be needed, however, "so that the EU can, *in addition to possible recourse to NATO capabilities,* have the best possible command and control resources at its disposal [emphasis added]." It was important to complete talks with NATO rapidly with regard to access to "NATO capabilities and assets."[14] Thus, at the outset, the Europeans were building in the possibility of some confusion about what "headquarters" would be used in particular circumstances.

---

[11]Ibid., paragraph 6.

[12]For example, Joint Exercise Study (JES 01) from June 11–15, 2001, hosted by the Netherlands Ministry of Defence was a WEU-led CJTF "exercise using NATO assets and capabilities and in particular requiring a CJTF Headquarters, under the political control and strategic direction of the WEU Council" (*NATO Press Release [2001]081,* June 5, 2001). In addition,

> A WEU/NATO Joint Crisis Management Exercise was held for the first time in February 2000, to test ESDI-related concepts and arrangements for handling WEU-led operations making use of NATO assets and capabilities (*NATO Handbook,* "Chapter 15: The Wider Institutional Framework for Security," op. cit.).

[13]Ibid., paragraph B. This point should be evaluated partly in terms of the possibility that the European rapid reaction force could act beyond Europe in areas where "NATO"—i.e., primarily the United States—chose not to be engaged, potentially in much of Africa.

[14]Ibid.

Chapter Fourteen

U.S. CONCERNS CRYSTALLIZE

The United States formally supported the Capabilities Commitment Conference; as Secretary Albright said, as "a strongly positive development we wholly support."[1] Notably, however, she added in her written statement that "This EU force will be available to both NATO and the EU."[2] This was true enough in terms of most, though not all, of the EU forces pledged at the conference; but "available to . . . NATO" is certainly not true of the European rapid reaction force itself; and this serious misperception only serves to underscore transatlantic disagreements about the development of ESDP. Indeed, the parallel development within NATO during the latter part of 2000—and especially the U.S. government—was focused solidly on the problem of capabilities: what the rapid reaction force would actually be able to do and, more to the point, what allies would be doing that could contribute directly to *NATO's* military capacities, especially through the Defense Capabilities Initiative.

During this period, capabilities were part of what was crystallizing as a triad of principal U.S. concerns. Lord Robertson, as NATO secretary general, effectively summarized these in an effort to bridge gaps of understanding and approach between his institution and the sister EU. As early as November 1999, he had sought to turn debate from the "three *D*'s" of the United States (in fact, as argued above, four

---

[1]"United States Backs European Rapid Reaction Force," Department of State, November 20, 2000.

[2]Ibid.

"*D*'s") to a set of positive formulations, which he called the "three *I*'s":

> For my part, I will ensure that ESDI is based on three key principles, the three *I*'s: *improvement* in European defense capabilities; *inclusiveness* and transparency for all Allies, and the *indivisibility* of transatlantic security, based on our shared values [emphasis added].[3]

In an apparent attempt to take a constructive approach, the United States readily seized upon this formulation.[4] In a joint article in the *Wall Street Journal Europe* in March 2000, Secretaries Albright and Cohen explicitly endorsed the three *I*'s—translating the third one as "indivisibility of security *structures* [emphasis added]."[5] On improving capabilities, they were clear and direct:

> New structures and commitments by themselves are not the answer to [the] challenge. Simply put, Europe needs more military capability. This will require spending more on defense, and spending smarter.[6]

---

[3]NATO, November 15, 1999, op. cit. Compare the first part of this statement with that of the French defense minister in February 2001: "what might damage the cohesion of the Alliance would be for Europeans to have failed to decide to improve their military capabilities" (Alain Richard, February 3, 2001, op. cit.).

[4]Of course, the three *I*'s do not cover all the territory of the three *D*'s, since "improvement in European defense capabilities" substitutes for avoiding "duplication" of existing efforts; and "indivisibility of transatlantic security" is not quite the same as "avoid preempting Alliance decision-making by de-linking ESDI from NATO."

[5]The two references to "indivisibility" are, of course, not identical. See Madeleine K. Albright and William S. Cohen, "Get ESDI Right: Europe Should Beef up Its Military Capabilities," *Wall Street Journal Europe*, March 24, 2000. Cohen also endorsed the three *I*'s at a WEU conference in Washington (in a session chaired by the author). But he was categorical about what this meant to him:

> We do not want to see a situation where it's [ESDI's] an EU solution not a NATO solution. The ESDI, the ESDP should be, generally speaking, under the umbrella of NATO itself; separable, but not separate (William S. Cohen, *Remarks to Western European Union's Transatlantic Forum*, Washington, D.C., June 28, 2000).

[6]Ibid.:

> Our European allies and partners need to improve the deployability and mobility of their forces, and ensure that they are able to survive, communicate, persevere and succeed in future engagements.

On inclusiveness, they argued that "Our NATO allies who are not members of the EU should have a voice in shaping the EU's security and defense deliberations." They did leave an out for the European Union by accepting that "final EU decisions are for the EU . . . [but] we encourage it to include the non-EU allies in its efforts."[7] "Encourage," of course, is not as strong a word as "insist," which could come into play if NATO were being asked to transfer assets to the EU for use under ESDP. And on "indivisibility of security structures," the two U.S. cabinet officials argued that "The closest possible links are necessary for NATO to be able to support an EU-led action where the Alliance is not engaged"; and they called for efforts to "create a concrete NATO-EU relationship that assures transparency and cooperation," so that "organizational decisions about future military operations will not be taken in isolation by either NATO or the EU."[8] This is an important concern, but also tactfully put, because it draws back from suggesting a "de-linking" of NATO and ESDI (or "decoupling," the extra *D* discussed earlier).

Secretary Cohen responded forcefully to EU decisions made at Santa Maria da Feira and the EU's subsequent efforts to develop both ESDP institutions and linkages with NATO. He did this at the NATO informal defense ministerial meeting in Birmingham on October 10, reiterating a number of U.S. positions—including that there be "no discrimination against any of the member states of either organization."[9] He said further:

Also Albright and Cohen noted that "The war in Kosovo showed a clear gap between U.S. and European military capability in the fields most relevant to modern warfare."

[7] Ibid.

[8] Ibid.

[9] This was one of four principles for the NATO-EU relationship, where:

- NATO and EU efforts to strengthen European security are coherent and mutually reinforcing;

- The autonomy and integrity of decision-making in both organizations are respected, each organization dealing with the other on an equal footing;

- Both organizations place a high premium on transparency, close and frequent contacts on a wide range of levels, and efforts that are complementary; and

Let me be clear on America's position; We agree with [the goal of a military capability to back up CFSP]—not grudgingly, not with resignation, but with wholehearted conviction. The notion that Europe must begin to prepare for an eventual American withdrawal from Europe has no foundation in fact or in policy . . . . It is overwhelmingly likely that in any situation where any Ally's involvement on a significant scale is justified and where there is a consensus in Europe to undertake a military operation, the United States would be part of the operation. In addition, it is difficult to imagine a situation in which the United States was prepared to participate, but our European Allies would prefer to act alone.[10]

Cohen's major points related to the relationship between the two organizations in terms of planning and, specifically, that it should be centered in NATO, not in the EU.[11] The European Union, he argued,

---

•   There is no discrimination against any of the member states of either organization (William S. Cohen, *Remarks at the NATO Informal Defense Ministerial*, October 10, 2000).

Cohen also advanced an interesting formulation:

The United States actively supports European efforts to increase and improve their contribution to collective defense and crisis response operations within NATO (*through the ESDI*), and to build a capability (through the ESDP) to act militarily under the EU where NATO as a whole is not engaged [emphasis added] (ibid.).

This unusual definition of ESDI clearly implies that the EU's efforts would somehow form a distinct part of NATO's capacities—perhaps an effort to hark back to the "separable but not separate" device from Berlin in 1996.

[10]Ibid.

[11]"Planning" has two basic aspects. "Operational planning" is just what the name implies: what the alliance does (through its commands) to get ready to conduct military actions. "Defense planning" is more long term and relates to the military goals and efforts of individual countries and the alliance as a whole. Among NATO nations, effort is measured against standards defined within the alliance. The key NATO instruments for defense planning are:

a.   Ministerial Guidance, issued every two years, followed by:

b.   Force Goals, covering a six year period, which are adopted every two years; and

c.   Annual Defence Review, leading to an agreed NATO force plan for the succeeding five year period, the first year of which is a firm commitment of forces to NATO by each nation (*NATO Logistics Handbook*, Chapter 4:

"should be able to count on NATO's operational and defense planning capabilities" in all circumstances, including "during an EU-led crisis response operation that does not use NATO capabilities and common assets." In short, for *operational* planning, NATO should be the locus:

> In the real world, if Europe were to face one or more crisis response operations, we are confident that priorities for how to apportion NATO operational planning resources will be self-evident to all concerned.[12] . . . [At the same time,] in regard to *defense planning* [emphasis added], which would not be directly affected by crisis operations, we would envision a unitary, coherent, and collaborative approach that meets the needs of both NATO and the EU. I could very well imagine this unitary approach taking the form of a "European Security and Defense Planning System," or "ESDPS."[13]

"Determination of Logistic Requirements and Logistic Support: Defence Planning Process," Section 403, October 1997).

A key element in the process is the allies' national force plans, which

> are forwarded to NATO Headquarters in the national responses to the annual Defence Planning Questionnaire (DPQ) and are analyzed by both the Military Authorities and the International Staff (IS). . . . The results of this examination are then passed to the DRC (Defense Review Committee) which attempts to eliminate any remaining differences in multilateral meetings at NATO Headquarters. All nations participate. . . . After these multilateral examinations, the DRC prepares a Country Chapter on each nation . . . setting out how far nations have been able to meet the Force Goals, and where and why shortfalls have occurred (ibid., Section 404).

Thus, each ally in effect subjects its own defense planning to review and critique by the rest of the Alliance, and the collective result is an attempt to create some coherence among allied militaries.

[12]Ibid.:

> We should not lose time arguing over highly improbable scenarios that are advanced with the intent of demonstrating that NATO operational planners somehow would be "overtaxed" by multiple crises and, therefore, unable to respond to EU requirements. After all, under existing Ministerial Guidance, NATO must have the capability to conduct up to three major operations, including two corps-sized crisis response operations, which implies of course that we must maintain a quite robust planning capability, which will not be overtaxed by concurrent operations.

[13]Ibid.

Indeed, he argued that

> It would be highly ineffective, seriously wasteful of resources, and contradictory to the basic principles of close NATO-EU cooperation . . . if [each] were to proceed along the path of relying on autonomous force planning structures.[14] [And to this end, he saw] no contradiction between the four non-NATO EU members gaining broad transparency into NATO defense planning, [and] the eight non-EU NATO members gaining reciprocal transparency into the EU headline goal process.[15]

Cohen made a further effort to reduce a point of potential complication—and political friction—over the development of ESDP by proposing to enlarge the role envisioned since Berlin in 1996 for NATO's Deputy Supreme Allied Commander Europe (DSACEUR).[16] At Berlin, it had been agreed that DSACEUR could serve as the WEU's "strategic commander," under the "separable but not separate" concept, if the WEU so desired. Cohen envisioned further work for "DSACEUR as the 'strategic coordinator' between NATO and the EU."[17] This would even apply during "an EU-led crisis response operation that does not use NATO assets." And Deputy SACEUR would serve as "force generator" for the EU during a crisis.[18] As with his

---

[14]Ibid.:

> It is hard to conceive of any argument based on logic, practicality, or effectiveness that European allies who are also EU members should proceed along separate defense planning tracks—one within NATO, the other within the EU—to prepare for the same range of crisis response options. The same reasoning applies to the four non-NATO EU members . . . [that] participate in the [NATO] Planning and Review Process. . . . It is hard to understand why they would be better off by creating a new, separate defense planning and operational planning track in the EU (ibid.).

[15]Ibid. Thus, under his proposal for an ESDPS, "Turkey, for example, would be present when the headline goals of EU countries are reviewed; similarly, Sweden . . . would have a seat at the table when the force goals of Allies are reviewed" (ibid.). This "sweetener"—trading a position for Turkey for a similar one for the non-NATO EU members—was a departure from past U.S. concerns about such intrusiveness into NATO business.

[16]DSACEUR British General Sir Rupert Smith was succeeded in 2001 by the Chief of Staff of Allied Command Europe, German General Dieter Stöckmann.

[17]Ibid.

[18]Ibid. Cohen argued that, with both his proposals for an ESDPS and the role of Deputy SACEUR, "we have no intention somehow to diminish the EU's capability for

proposal for a joint planning system, this proposal would appear logical, at least to military experts, and it would decrease complications both for NATO and for any circumstances in which a strictly Europeans-only operation transmuted into a requirement for NATO military action. But it would also reduce the sense of "autonomy" of EU/ESDP prized by some European countries, especially France, and this point could not have been lost on the supporters of an EU, under ESDP, able to make "autonomous decisions."

Lest any of his points were lost on his audience, in press commentary immediately following the Birmingham informal defense ministerial meeting, Cohen underscored that the reason "why the United States strongly supports the European Security and Defense Program [sic]" was not for its own sake, but because together NATO's DCI and the ESDP "give members of the alliance and the EU an opportunity to plan and work together to create a more modern defense structure." Indeed, "As EU members meet the headline goal of creating a rapidly deployable and sustainable combat force, it will also enhance NATO's capability"[19]—in effect, doing double duty and drawing on the added political incentive provided by ESDP for modernizing European defenses.

Cohen went on to stress the importance of the DCI goals and that what the EU does through ESDP must be consistent with those goals:

> So that we do not have separate capabilities, in terms of being inconsistent and non-compatible. . . . And, we also have one set of planners. What we don't want to see is a separate planning bureaucracy established that is independent and separate from that of NATO itself. . . . [In sum, the] U.S. supports ESDI/P, *provided it is consistent with NATO requirements and responsibilities* [emphasis added].[20]

But Cohen's strongest—and bluntest—comments came at the time of the December 2000 NATO defense ministers' meetings in Brussels,

---

independent decision and direction, which understandably would include planning *at a strategic level* [emphasis added]" (ibid.). Of course, these arrangements would have precisely the effect of diminishing independent direction.

[19]William S. Cohen, *Press Conference*, Birmingham, England, October 10, 2000.

[20]Ibid.

a few days before the EU's European Council summit in Nice. On his way to the NATO meetings, his last as U.S. defense secretary, he stressed his two cardinal points: capabilities and a unified planning process. On the former, "make sure that the headline goals are met and make sure that whatever is done for ESDP is consistent with the DCI."[21] And on the latter, if the Europeans want "a separate operational planning capability . . . from [that of] NATO itself, then that is going to weaken the ties between the United States and NATO and NATO and the EU."[22] There was no mincing of words in Brussels. Commenting publicly on what he had said in private to the NATO defense ministers:

> As long as there is openness, transparency and a non-competitive relationship [between NATO and EU/ESDP], then the United States will remain committed [to the NATO Alliance]. But if, in fact, the capabilities that were identified as being needed are not filled—if, in fact, we only have verbal commitments or lip service being paid to developing capabilities—if, in fact, we have a competing institution that is established, then it would be inconsistent with military effectiveness. If, in fact, there was any element of using the force structure in a way to simply to set up a way to set up [sic] a competing headquarters, a competitive headquarters not being the most militarily efficient or desirable. If all of these factors are not taken into account, *then NATO could become a relic of the past* [emphasis added].[23]

---

[21]William S. Cohen, *Briefing En Route to NATO Defense Ministers' Meeting,* December 4, 2000.

[22]Ibid. On this occasion, he seemed to separate defense planning from operational planning. He continued:

> That's something, I think the overwhelming majority do not want to see take place. They want to see ESDP to strengthen NATO itself. So, I think this is not the case of me pushing against a closed door, but an open door, that this is something that they see very much in their own interest.

[23]He continued:

> That is not something that the United States desires and it is not something that we foresee but so long as we can see the warning flags and the caveats, and say that the deeds must measure up to the words that we've all signed up to, that the capabilities identified in the DCI and within the Strategic Concept are, in fact, measured up to—whether they're called ESDP or DCI—so as long as they have capabilities instead of bureaucracies, then NATO will continue to play a vital role in European security. That's basically the formu-

No senior U.S. administration official had gone so far before in publicly criticizing ESDP—indeed, in laying on the line NATO's very future. Cohen went on (in a separate interview) to repeat his proposal for a 23-nation single defense planning process, indicating that "it would prove a flexible and generous approach to participation by non-EU allies."[24] Most important:

> If NATO and the EU with its ESDP are seen as autonomous and competing institutions, rather than integrated, transparent and complementary ones, then NATO and collective security are likely to suffer, leaving North America and Europe alike to relay on uncoordinated, inefficient and ad hoc responses to destabilizing threats.[25]

In the same vein, Cohen hit hard on the issue of defense budgets:

> What also has to be of concern . . . is that a number of allies are going in the opposite direction. Namely their budgets are remaining flat, or some are even decreasing in real terms.[26]

---

lation of what I said [to the ministers] (William S. Cohen, *DoD News Briefing* [with Ukrainian Minister of Defense Gen. Oleksandr Ivanovych Kuzmuk], Brussels, December 5, 2000).

There were also reports that, in the defense ministers' meeting, Cohen had warned "of a developing 'EU caucus' in NATO." Richard Norton-Taylor, *The Guardian*, December 7, 2000 (www.guardian.co.uk/eu/story/0,7369,407956,00.html).

[24]William S. Cohen, *Transcript of Press Conference,* Brussels, December 5, 2000.

[25]Ibid. In this press conference, Cohen agreed that his word "relic" could be replaced by Lord Robertson's word "irrelevant":

> It means the same thing. . . . We must have new capabilities, consistent capabilities, so that we operate effectively together and not have duplicative or redundant planning and operational planning institutions (ibid.).

[26]Ibid. He also added:

> Well there are a number of things that individual countries can do. They certainly can reform and reshape their military. Some will get smaller, but more mobile, more quickly deployable, more sustainable as such. All of the goals have been identified in the DCI. That can be done through some restructuring, some can be done through base closures, and consolidations which we have been through in the United States and which we need to go through in addition to achieve more savings. Some can be achieved through cooperative measures by joint efforts to procure certain specific items. Some can be done through transatlantic cooperation. But as I pointed out in my remarks to the NATO members today, you cannot achieve the goals of the DCI,

And he reiterated his position of opposing discrimination against non-EU members of NATO, because, if so,

> then you run the risk of having a line, a division, which can cause fragmentation and a loss of that cohesion which is so critical to having a unified position for NATO members.[27]

By the time he had finished his list of criticisms, therefore, the U.S. defense secretary had made quite clear that ESDP had to pass certain clear tests—or both NATO and the transatlantic relationship would suffer. It was the moment of maximum transatlantic strain over the development of the European pillar of the alliance.

---

through savings alone. There must be increases in spending. That is going to be required if we are going to do what we have to do in terms of achieving those goals. So a good deal can be done by purchasing off the shelf technology, commercially available technology, joining in some sort of joint ventures as such in terms of sharing the resources necessary to acquire certain types of capability. But ultimately, there has to be a commitment to defense spending and increases in that spending (ibid.).

[27]Ibid.

Chapter Fifteen

NICE AND BEYOND

In terms of developing confidence in the United States about the future of ESDP, the European Council that convened at Nice two days after Cohen's comments was important as much for what it did not do as for what it did. First, it accomplished several major steps forward in developing the institutions for the European Security and Defense Policy—designed "to enable the European Union to assume its responsibilities for crisis management as a whole."[1] These steps focused on the elaboration of the Political and Security Committee (PSC), the Military Committee of the European Union (EUMC), and the Military Staff of the European Union (EUMS). The composition, structure, duties, and operations of each were spelled out in great detail—indeed, to a detail rarely seen even in descriptions of the workings of comparable NATO bodies.[2] To be sure, these elaborations were carefully embedded in what, since Helsinki a year earlier, was now-standard language about

> where NATO as a whole is not engaged. . . . This does not involve the
> establishment of a European army. . . . NATO remains the basis for
> the collective defence of its members and will continue to play an

---

[1] See Nice European Council, *Presidency Conclusions,* December 7–9, 2000, "Annex VI, On the European Security and Defence Policy, II. Establishment of Permanent Political and Military Structures."

[2] Ibid. The document also made a number of other significant decisions, including for civilian aspects of crisis management. Notably, the EU "confirmed its intention of itself assuming the crisis-management function of the WEU." This included the creation of a satellite center and an institute for security studies to incorporate existing WEU bodies. Ibid., "Annex VI, V. Inclusion in the EU of the Appropriate Functions of the WEU."

important role in crisis management. The development of the ESDP will contribute to the vitality of a renewed Transatlantic link . . . lead[ing] to a genuine strategic partnership between the EU and NATO in the management of crises with due regard for the two organisations' decision-making autonomy [etc.].[3]

In noting the results of the Capabilities Commitments Conference on November 20, Nice also "signalled [the member states'] determination to make the necessary efforts to improve their operational capabilities further,"[4] focusing on "command and control, intelligence and strategic air and naval transport capabilities"[5]—three areas where, under Berlin and Berlin-plus, the Europeans would have to rely heavily on NATO (and also the United States).

Notably, as well, the Nice council meeting stressed the cooperation that had been built up with NATO during 2000, especially on "the principles for consultation, cooperation and transparence [sic] with NATO and the modalities for EU access to NATO assets and capabilities (Berlin plus)."[6] But it also stressed that the burden of continuing effort lay with NATO: "The EU hopes for a favourable reaction from NATO so that these arrangements can be implemented on a mutu-

---

[3]Ibid., "Introduction." The document also was careful to introduce a principle that had bedeviled NATO at the time of the Kosovo Conflict: "The efforts made will enable Europeans in particular to respond more effectively and more coherently to requests from leading organisations such as the UN or the OSCE" (ibid.). This related to the issue of "mandate" for action. NATO had faced the problem of embarking on what it considered to be necessary military action in regard to Kosovo, for moral as well as political reasons, but could not obtain the formal blessing either from the OSCE or the United Nations Security Council, under Chapter VII of the UN Charter. This was deeply troubling to many European countries, viewing the problem against the background of experience, in particular from the first half of the 20th century. In the end, NATO worked out a compromise whereby each member state decided for itself the juridical basis for the "mandate"; but few were happy with the compromise; and the language cited here, while not "prohibitive"—that is, it does not limit EU action through ESDP to "requests" from "leading organisations"—the implication is clear that that would be the preferred course. The point was reinforced with what, on other occasions, would seem to be just "boilerplate" language: "The European Union recognises the primary responsibility of the United Nations Security Council for maintaining peace and international security" (ibid.).

[4]Ibid., "I. The Development of Military Capabilities and the Strengthening of Civil Crisis Management Capabilities: (1) Elaboration of the headline goal and of the military capability goals established in Helsinki."

[5]Ibid.

[6]Ibid., "IV. Permanent Arrangements for EU-NATO Consultation and Cooperation."

ally satisfactory basis"; and it laid a heavy emphasis on what NATO could provide:

> The EU reiterates the importance which it attaches to being able, when necessary, to make use of the assured access to NATO's planning capabilities and to the presumption of availability of NATO's assets and capabilities.[7] . . . [Further, the EU noted that member states concerned, i.e. NATO allies] will also deploy existing defence planning procedures, including, if appropriate, those of NATO and of the planning and review process (PARP) of the Partnership for Peace.[8]

This—in the realm of what Nice did *not* do—was about as close as the European Council came to acknowledging both Secretary Cohen's criticisms of the ESDP's potential planning mechanisms or his proposal for a European Security and Defense Planning System. Indeed, in one of the complex annexes to the Nice *Presidency Conclusions*, the EU member states clearly drew a distinction between situations where NATO assets and capabilities would be involved and where they would not be. In the former instance, "operational planning will be carried out by the Alliance's planning bodies," but "for an autonomous EU operation it will be carried out within one of the European strategic level headquarters." In the former case, non-EU European allies would be involved in planning according to NATO procedures. But in the latter case, where these non-EU NATO allies "are invited to take part," they (and candidates to join the EU) could send "liaison officers . . . for exchanges of information on operational planning and the contributions [by them] envisaged."[9]

---

[7]Ibid. It went on to say: "When the Union examines options with a view to an operation, the establishing of its strategic military options can involve a contribution by NATO's planning capabilities."

[8]Ibid., "EU Review Mechanism Goals," paragraph 5.

[9]Ibid., "Annex VI to Annex VI, Arrangements Concerning Non-EU European NATO Members and Other Countries Which Are Candidates for Accession to the EU, III. Arrangements During Crisis Periods: (B) Operations Phase." The European Union Military Staff Organisation would have "three main operational functions: early warning, situation assessment and strategic planning." On the last named, "It carries out the military aspects of strategic advance planning for Petersberg missions." And in crisis management situations, it defines initial broad options, among other things: "drawing as appropriate on planning support from external sources which will analyse

This one formulation carried a double worry for various NATO allies. For the United States (and others concerned about the coherence of NATO and its relations with the EU/ESDP), the operational planning functions were clearly to be contingent on the type of operation being undertaken, and in particular whether NATO assets were or were not to be requested: a step, it could be argued, that would or would not be taken well down the line after serious planning had already taken place. From NATO's point of view, the process was backwards: It should be joint planning first, then deciding who would undertake an operation (NATO or the European Union), then considering whether NATO assets would be needed and hence transferred, and then undertaking any subsequent planning—but again, from NATO's point of view, not done by any body not fully, regularly, and consistently "transparent" to NATO planners and procedures. To put the point even more directly: This issue of the locus of planning could create a serious impediment to making decisions on the basis of the agreed principle of "where NATO as a whole is not engaged." That bridge could not be crossed until NATO had a chance to review a situation, plan for it, and then judge whether it would or would not be engaged; the ESDP proposal for a bifurcated planning system presupposed that the "NATO engaged" issue had been decided even before the locus for planning could be agreed upon.[10] Furthermore, by EU reasoning, there was to be a one-way street in practice:

> In the field of operational planning, the Military Staff of the [NATO] Alliance with responsibility for handling EU requests will be accessible to experts from the Member States who also wish without discrimination.[11]

---

and further develop these options in more detail" (ibid., "Annex V to Annex VI, European Union Military Staff Organisation, 4. Functions").

[10]The EU proposals for consultations with NATO in the event of a crisis also have a highly cumbersome quality that raised questions about whether they could work in "the real world" or would exist more for show than substance. See ibid., "Annex VII to Annex VI, Standing Arrangements for Consultation and Cooperation Between the EU and NATO, III. NATO/EU Relations in Times of Crisis, (A) and (B)."

[11]Ibid., "Appendix to Annex VII to Annex VI, Annex to the Permanent Arrangement on EU/NATO Consultation and Cooperation on the Implementation of Paragraph 10 of the Washington Communiqué, (1) Guaranteed Access to NATO's Planning Capabilities."

There was nothing about a reciprocal right for NATO in regard to any EU planning, including that conducted by national headquarters. In all, no serious military strategist or planner could endorse such a set of procedures for two institutions that sought to be able to work together.

This ESDP planning formulation at Nice also had particular implications for "non-EU NATO members," of which Turkey was most concerned and most vocal. By the same logic as that above, the decision about whether a country like Turkey were to be engaged in an EU-led operation would come relatively late in the day, in terms of the overall process. Thus,

> once the EU begins to examine in depth an option requiring the use of NATO assets and capabilities, particular attention will be paid to consultation of the six non-EU European NATO members.[12] [Furthermore, it would only be after] . . . the Council has chosen the strategic military option(s) [that] the operational planning work will be presented to the non-EU European NATO members . . . to enable them to determine the nature and volume of the contribution they could make.[13]

Only then might the outsiders be invited to take part in an operation;[14] they would be able to take part in a committee of contributors, to "play a key role in the day-to-day management of the operation,"[15] although it would be the Political and Security Committee that would exercise "the political control and strategic direction of the operation," but which would "take account of the views expressed by the Committee of Contributors."[16]

There is, of course, method in all of these procedures.[17] But for Turkey, already bruised by its sense of exclusion from membership in

---

[12]Ibid., "(A) Pre-Operational Phase."

[13]Ibid., "(B) Operational Phase."

[14]Ibid.

[15]Ibid., "(C) Committee of Contributors."

[16]Ibid.

[17]One of the most torturous related to the review mechanism for military capabilities (ibid., "Appendix to Annex I to Annex VI, Achievement of the Headline Goal . . . Principles"):

the European Union (despite having notionally been put on the list of prospective entrants at the Helsinki European Council summit meeting in December 1999), these arrangements smacked very much of another form of exclusion—by bureaucratic process. Furthermore, without full engagement in what the EU was doing, Turkey might find that an operation were being conducted in a contiguous region, affecting its interests, but without its active participation in all phases. Thus, as noted earlier, at the NATO foreign ministers' meeting in Brussels on December 14–15, 2000, Turkey placed a hold on completing work within NATO on developing cooperative arrangements with the EU, under ESDP. Although a wide range of these arrangements were in fact agreed upon and pledges made about completing permanent arrangements between NATO and the EU,[18]

> Concerning relations with third countries: (1) the mechanism will ensure that the contributions of European States which are members of NATO but not part of the EU, and of the application countries, are taken into account, in order to enable an evaluation to be made of their complementary commitments which contribute to the improvement of European capabilities, and to facilitate their possible participation in EU-led operations in accordance with the Helsinki and Feira decisions.

However, any such contributions of forces by states such as these "will be examined, in conjunction with the nations concerned, on the basis of the same criteria as those applying to Member States' contributions" (ibid., "Relations with Third Countries").

[18]Ministerial Meeting of the North Atlantic Council, *Final Communiqué*, NATO Headquarters, Brussels, NATO Release M-NAC-2(2000)1124, December 14–15, 2000, paragraph 33:

> Subject to this [principle that nothing is agreed until everything is agreed], we intend to put in place arrangements for: assured EU access to NATO planning capabilities able to contribute to military planning for EU-led operations; the presumption of availability to the EU of pre-identified NATO capabilities and common assets for use in EU-led operations; the identification of a range of European command options for EU-led operations, further developing the role of Deputy SACEUR in order for him to assume fully and effectively his European responsibilities; and the further adaptation of the Alliance's defence planning system, taking account of relevant activities in and proposals from the European Union. Allies will be consulted on the EU's proposed use of assets and capabilities, prior to the decision to release these assets and capabilities, and kept informed during the operation.

Also, ibid., paragraph 31:

> Furthermore, [regarding permanent arrangements on meetings and consultations, etc.] to ensure full transparency, consultation and co-operation between NATO and the EU . . . , the Alliance agrees that these proposals

NATO "proceeded on the principle that nothing will be agreed until everything is agreed—the participation issue is also relevant in this context";[19] and the issue of EU access to NATO planning was the linchpin. The practical effect was that the complex efforts to elaborate—or overly elaborate—ESDP institutions had produced a political setback in relations with at least one NATO country, which probably had more covert support among other allies than its apparent isolation indicated. Notably, the EU's silence on Secretary Cohen's proposal for workable planning cooperation could be expected to color U.S. thinking about a supposed Turkish "obstruction."[20]

Furthermore, the United States could not be oblivious to internal differences within the European Union. Thus, the French continued to nibble at the edges of existing agreements. At Nice, for instance, President Chirac reportedly argued that the Headline Goal Task Force "should be independent from NATO's military headquarters." But, according to the same sources, under British pressure he later said that "EU efforts were intended to 'complement' NATO."[21] Notably, from the perspective of a U.S. government seeking to line

---

constitute the basis for the permanent NATO/EU agreement. We stand ready to work to finalise this agreement without delay.

[19]Ibid. The communiqué stated further that:

We underline, as we did at the Washington Summit and subsequent Ministerial meetings, the importance of finding solutions satisfactory to all Allies to the issue of participation. We note the provisions agreed by the European Council at Nice for dialogue, consultation and co-operation with non-EU European Allies on issues related to security and defence policy and crisis management and as well as the modalities for participation in EU-led military operations. We welcome the commitment to intensify consultation in times of crisis, which will also enable non-EU European Allies to raise their concerns when they consider their security interests might be involved. It is particularly important in this context that non-EU European Allies can request meetings with the European Union and submit proposals for agenda items (ibid., paragraph 32).

[20]However, at the EU-U.S. summit in Washington, D.C., on December 18, the communiqué said simply on this point that "the U.S. notes with appreciation the arrangements offered by the EU for its relationship with NATO European allies." See European Union, *Highlights of EU-U.S. Cooperation Under the New Transatlantic Agenda*, December 18, 2000, www.europa.eu.int/comm/external_relations/us/summit12_00/nta.htm.

[21]See Ian Black, "Chirac Gives Way in Row with Blair on NATO," *The Guardian*, December 9, 2000, www.guardian.co.uk/Print/0,3858,4102882,00.html.

up European support for its position, it was perhaps fortuitous that the British Conservative Party took on the Blair government over ESDP, thus seeming to stiffen the position of the British government in tilting toward its American connection as opposed to that with France.[22]

---

[22]See, for example, Sir John Weston, "EU Defence Force 'Could Lead to the Break-up of NATO,'" *Daily Telegraph*, January 11, 2001; Alexander Nicoll, "European Force 'No Rival to NATO,'" *Financial Times*, November 30, 2000; and Ben Fenton and George Jones, "Pentagon Chief Sends for Tory," *Daily Telegraph*, February 17, 2001. This last article is remarkable less for its reportage on concerns expressed in the Pentagon and on Capitol Hill about ESDP than for what it says about the *Telegraph's* part in British party politics on this issue.

Chapter Sixteen

THE NEW U.S. ADMINISTRATION

With the onset of any new U.S. administration, for a time progress in U.S.-European relations comes to a virtual standstill. The allies want time to take the measure of the new U.S. president and his team; and the new team will itself take time, both to be constituted (the appointment and confirmation processes are long and drawn out) and to revisit old propositions about security relations with Europe before, almost always, ratifying at least most of what the last administration has done.[1] This time, there was also virtue in a breathing space in the development of relations between NATO and EU/ESDP, given that the latter institution had been developing at such a breakneck speed (and still needs to sort out many of its own internal relationships, in both theory and practice), and given that no one could yet predict for certain how those ESDP-NATO procedures already agreed upon—or provisionally so, subject to the "principle" that nothing is agreed upon until all is agreed upon—would actually work.

But two things were clear by the beginning of 2001: The European Union had moved far and fast in the direction of creating a military institution that would have the capacity for autonomous *decision*—if not, in fact, yet much autonomous *action*—and the rise of this institution was posing some complex problems for NATO and for its

---

[1]This has also happened in the George W. Bush administration, as testified to by the president's speech at Warsaw University on June 15, 2001: It could very likely have been given word for word, in terms of policy, by his predecessor, President Clinton. See The White House, Office of the Press Secretary, *Remarks by the President in Address to Faculty and Students of Warsaw University*, Warsaw, June 15, 2001.

sense of primacy. In particular, there was a special point of procedure: When, in the development of a crisis and the response to it by
both NATO and the EU (with the latter having a capacity that the
former lacks for civilian/diplomatic as well as military crisis management), would it become relevant to pose the question whether
the alliance as a "whole" would or would not be "engaged?" Indeed,
the development of any but the most clear-cut crises, in terms of
magnitude and palpable challenge, would likely be so ambiguous
that the CFSP and ESDP mechanisms would be well into play before
NATO would become formally seized of a need to be involved. Its
primacy, therefore, might have to be regained, or asserted, or simply
conceded by default, after another institution was already exercising
its responsibilities. This is a ready-made formula for "competition"
in practice if not in theory.

Early indications of thinking in the new Bush administration came at
the beginning of February 2001, when the new secretary of defense,
Donald H. Rumsfeld (who had served before as both defense secretary and as ambassador to NATO, 1973–74), attended the annual
Munich Conference on European Security Policy. In his brief address, he noted, appropriately, that he was "not yet as knowledgeable
enough to discuss [ESDI] in great detail." But he did have some basic
beliefs—which mirrored those of the preceding administration, in
particular with regard to NATO's core importance, to efforts that
strengthen it, to problems of duplication or those that could "per-
turb" the transatlantic link, and to the importance that all NATO
allies wanting to take part in ESDI activities should be able to do so:

> Our European allies and partners know that NATO is at the heart of
> Europe's defenses. Therefore, to sustain our past success into the
> future we must first and foremost maintain NATO as the core of
> Europe's security structures for Europe. I favor efforts that
> strengthen NATO. What happens within our Alliance and what
> happens to it must comport with its continued strength, resilience,
> and effectiveness. Actions that could reduce NATO's effectiveness
> by confusing duplication or by perturbing the transatlantic link
> would not be positive. Indeed they run the risk of injecting instabil-
> ity into an enormously important Alliance. And . . . whatever shape

the effort may finally take . . . it should be inclusive—open to all NATO members who wish to take part.[2]

Furthermore, Rumsfeld stressed two other key U.S. themes to reporters traveling with him: the need for increases in real European military capabilities and a planning process that works:

> If I saw more dollars coming in, in budgets that would net increase the strength of NATO nations, that would be encouraging. I have not seen that. I am more interested in addition than subtraction. . . . I [also] think the planning process would be terribly important, to the extent it were separate. I think you could end up with the gears not meshing well, and to the extent it was common, I think that the gears conceivably would mesh better.[3]

These were preliminary positions of the new U.S. administration; but they tracked with what its predecessor had suggested as touchstones for judging the development of ESDP.

The first top-level commentary came during a visit to the United States by British Prime Minister Blair—now fully cognizant of the role that his position on ESDP would play in his impending national reelection campaign: Just as he had embraced ESDP fully at St. Mâlo in December 1998 in part as a surrogate for Britain's abstention from the Euro, so it could be argued that Tory questioning about UK support for ESDP had become a surrogate for the same broader debate on the Euro and Britain's overall relationship within the European Union.

The two leaders exchanged ritual—but critical—pledges. President Bush said that the British prime minister

> assured me that NATO is going to be the primary way to keep the peace in Europe, and . . . I assured him the United States will be

---

[2]"Remarks as Delivered by Secretary of Defense Donald H. Rumsfeld," Munich, Germany, February 3, 2001.

[3]"Media Availability with Secretary Rumsfeld en Route to Munich, Germany," *DefenseLINK*, February 2, 2001.

actively engaged in NATO, remain engaged in Europe with our allies.[4]

But the two leaders went further:

> He [Blair] also assured me [Bush] that the European defense would no way undermine NATO. He also assured me that there would be a joint command, that planning would take place within NATO, and that should all NATO not wish to go on a mission, that would then serve as a catalyst for the defense forces moving on their own. And finally, I was very hopeful when we discussed the Prime Minister's vision that such a vision would encourage our NATO allies and friends to bolster their defense budgets, perhaps.[5]

For his part, Prime Minister Blair noted:

> the important thing to remember is that, as the President has just outlined to you, this [the employment of EU/ESDP forces] is in circumstances where NATO as a whole chooses not to be engaged; it is limited to the peacekeeping and humanitarian tasks that are set out. It is not a standing army, it is a capability that Europe should have. . . . But where NATO as a whole chooses not to be engaged, it is important that we have the capability, where it's right and within these limited tasks that I've set out, to be able to act, should we choose to do so ourselves. And I think, done in that way, it is something that can strengthen NATO, give us an additional string to our bow in circumstances where NATO doesn't want to be involved. And I think the President is absolutely right in a sense to put it up to us in Europe and say, well, if we are going to do this, then let us make sure that our capabilities match our aspirations.[6]

Notable in this exchange are the British pledge about "where NATO as a whole chooses not to be engaged"; the emphasis on capabilities;

---

[4]The White House, Office of the Press Secretary, *Remarks by the President and Prime Minister Blair in Joint Press Conference,* Green Top Camp Dining Hall, Camp David, Maryland, February 23, 2001.

[5]Ibid. President Bush was incorrect in saying that "there would be a joint [NATO-EU] command" and also that "planning would take place within NATO." Neither has been agreed upon.

[6]Ibid. Blair was incorrect in saying that ESDP would be limited to "peacekeeping and humanitarian tasks." In theory, as discussed earlier, Petersberg Tasks could go further.

and one apparent misunderstanding by President Bush of what was then the prevailing situation—the idea that "planning would take place within NATO"—and a misstatement: "that there would be a joint command." Not clear, however, is whether these last two statements represented misperceptions by Bush of what Blair had told him; or a lapse in Blair's presentation—which clearly happened when he implicitly ruled out the most ambitious of the Petersberg Tasks: "tasks of combat forces in crisis management, including *peacemaking* [emphasis added]."[7] But these matters do underscore the continued problem of communication across the Atlantic about ESDP—what it will do and what it will not do—as well as the slippery business of which European states want what from this new venture, and which European states find themselves caught between visions broadly represented by France, on the one hand, and most of the rest of the alliance on the other.

A month later, the new administration had the chance to try pinning down Germany—often the "swing ally" in relations between France and the United States, although careful, whenever possible, not to have to choose between them. In a written statement in Washington on March 29, German Chancellor Gerhard Schroeder and President Bush endorsed ESDP

---

[7] *Title V: Provisions on a Common Foreign and Security Policy.* Maastricht (*The Single European Act of 1992*) laid out the framework for CFSP and set as a goal "the eventual framing of a common defence policy, which might in time lead to a common defence" (Article J.4.1). The WEU was asked "to elaborate and implement decisions and actions of the Union which have defence implications" (Article J.4.2). However, member state obligations under the North Atlantic Treaty were respected, and EU policy was to be "compatible with the common security and defence policy established within that [North Atlantic Treaty] framework" (Article J.4.4) At the same time, the Maastricht Treaty's "Final Act" included a declaration by the then nine members of the WEU that the "Member States of WEU welcome the development of the European security and defence identity" (ibid.). Thus the term ESDI was launched.

The Amsterdam Treaty went beyond Maastricht, referring to the "progressive framing of a common defence policy . . . which might lead to a common defence, should the European Council so decide" (paragraph 17.1, Title V of the Consolidated Version of the Treaty on European Union). Amsterdam provided for "the possibility of the integration of the WEU into the Union, should the European Council so decide" (ibid.). Also, "The progressive framing of a common defence policy will be supported, as Member States consider appropriate, by cooperation between them in the field of armaments" (ibid.). In addition, when the EU used the WEU "to elaborate and implement decisions of the Union," all member states would be "entitled to participate fully in the tasks in question" (ibid., paragraph 17.3). That meant inclusion of EU members that are not also members of NATO.

as an important contribution to sharing the burden of security and peace which will strengthen the Atlantic Alliance, . . . [and they welcomed] the efforts of the European Union to assume greater responsibility for crisis management by strengthening capabilities and developing the ability to take actions where NATO as a whole chooses not to engage.[8]

They also agreed that EU capabilities should be developed "in a manner that is fully coordinated, compatible, and transparent with NATO"; that there should be "the fullest possible participation by non-EU European NATO members in the operational planning and execution of EU-led exercises and operations"; and that ESDP also means "improv[ing] Europe's capabilities and enabl[ing] the EU to act where NATO as a whole is not engaged."[9] This statement provided the United States with much of what it wanted—although it was silent on contentious issues like planning. Also, on "participation by non-EU European NATO members," the qualifier "fullest possible" did not, on the face of it, resolve Turkish concerns.[10] As well, the Chancellor preempted another key U.S. concern: capabilities, and especially the fall in the German defense budget. Schroeder countered by describing everything else that Germany does to contribute to European security.[11]

---

[8]U.S. Department of State, "Bush-Schroeder Statement on Transatlantic Vision for 21st Century," *Washington File,* March 29, 2001.

[9]Ibid.

[10]See also U.S. State Department, "Background Briefing by Senior Administration Official on President's Meeting with Chancellor Schroeder of Germany," *Washington File,* March 29, 2001:

The Chancellor wanted to explain to the President that the concern expressed by some Americans that this [ESDP] is somehow intended by the Europeans as a competitor to NATO, or to weaken NATO, or to undermine NATO, to do something bad to NATO is not the case. And he said quite forcefully, this is the German position. . . . And our position . . . is that the United States supports and welcomes ESDP, provided it does what the Chancellor said it does.

[11]Ibid.:

The Chancellor . . . did make the point that Germany's contribution to European security and the definition of security should be seen more broadly. He said, you shouldn't just look at our military budget, you should look at what we've done to integrate the former East Germany; look what we've done to try to help bring democracy to Russia. These are also related

President Bush's trip to Europe in June 2001 provided a further occasion for repeating the key themes of the emerging relationship. Following a brief summit meeting with the other NATO heads of state and government in Brussels on June 13, the president summarized his interpretation of allied discussion:

> We agreed that NATO and the European Union must work in common purpose. It is in NATO's interest for the European Union to develop a rapid reaction capability. A strong, capable European force integrated with NATO would give us more options for handling crises when NATO, as a whole, chooses not to engage. NATO must be generous in the help it gives the EU. And similarly, the EU must welcome participation by NATO allies who are not members of the EU. And we must not waste scarce resources, duplicating effort or working at cross purposes. Our work together in the Balkans shows how much the 23 nations of NATO and the EU can achieve when we combine our efforts.[12]

Notable, of course, was the president's reference to a "capable European force integrated with NATO," with its sense of "separable but not separate" military capabilities.

A day later, however, the joint statement of the United States and the European Union from the Göteborg summit—the first-ever summit

---

to European security, and we're making a tremendous contribution. We're also contributing through the EU to the unification of Europe through EU enlargement.

[12]The White House, Office of the Press Secretary, *Press Availability with President Bush and NATO Secretary General Lord Robertson*, NATO Headquarters, Brussels, June 13, 2001. He also underscored the Balkans commitment, a point on which there had been some European doubts—an underscoring not irrelevant to issues of ESDI-ESDP:

> Our work together in the Balkans reminds me that I'm going to commit to the line that Colin Powell said: We came in together, and we will leave together. It is the pledge of our government, and it's a pledge that I will keep.

Further, he touched on the transatlantic defense market:

> It shouldn't be a question of whether to buy American or buy European, it should be a question of how to buy transatlantic. North American and European companies should collaborate to produce the most advanced systems at the lowest costs (ibid.).

President Bush was not correct in referring to a "European force integrated with NATO." The EU rapid reaction force would not, in fact, have this relationship to NATO.

of a U.S. president with all of the heads of state and government of the EU—left it to the United States to mark the central issues, without EU endorsement:

> The U.S. welcomes . . . [etc.,] where NATO as a whole is not engaged, and in a manner that is fully coordinated, where NATO interests are involved, and transparent with NATO, and that provides for the fullest possible participation of non-EU European allies.[13]

And in Warsaw, one day after the EU summit, President Bush repeated his formulation: "We welcome a greater role for the EU in European security, *properly integrated with NATO* [emphasis added]."[14]

---

[13]The White House, Office of the Press Secretary, *Göteborg Statement, Summit of the United States of America and the European Union,* Göteborg, Sweden, June 14, 2001. The full paragraph:

> The EU is working to acquire a civilian and military crisis management capability, which will reinforce the Union's ability to contribute to international peace and security in accordance with the principles of the UN Charter and make the EU a stronger, more capable partner in deterring and managing crises, thereby also enhancing the security of the Transatlantic Community. The U.S. welcomes the efforts of the EU to strengthen its capabilities and to develop the ability to manage crises, including through military operations, where NATO as a whole is not engaged, and in a manner that is fully coordinated, where NATO interests are involved, and transparent with NATO, and that provides for the fullest possible participation of non-EU European allies. In particular, the commitments made by the EU Member States concerning military capabilities will, as they are implemented, strengthen both the EU and the European pillar of the Atlantic Alliance (ibid.).

[14]The White House, Office of the Press Secretary, *Remarks by the President in Address to Faculty and Students of Warsaw University,* Warsaw, Poland, June 15, 2001:

> All nations should understand that there is no conflict between membership in NATO and membership in the European Union. My nation welcomes the consolidation of European unity, and the stability it brings. We welcome a greater role for the EU in European security, properly integrated with NATO.

The reference to "no conflict between membership" could have related, in part, to the pressures that some EU aspirant nations have been put under to show preference to the EU's activities in ESDP over NATO.

Chapter Seventeen

SORTING IT OUT

By the spring of 2001, work was moving forward both at the European Union and regarding the common understanding of the key areas of difference between the EU's ESDP and NATO, especially as seen from Washington. Progress in relations between the two institutions took place despite the restraints imposed by Turkey on actions by the North Atlantic Council, along with clear emphasis on the principle that "nothing is decided until all is decided." NATO and the EU began the practical work related to the four working groups and, on February 5, held the first-ever meeting of the North Atlantic Council with the EU's Political and Security Committee (PSC), at the ambassadorial level.[1] This was pursuant to an informal exchange of letters in January, between the Swedish EU presidency and the NATO secretary general, "confirming permanent arrangements for consultation and co-operation."[2] Ambassadors of the two institutions would meet six times a year, and foreign ministers twice.[3] Part of the

---

[1] Between then and the end of May, the two sets of ambassadors met four times. See Ministerial Meeting of the North Atlantic Council, *Final Communiqué*, Budapest, NATO Press Release M-NAC-1(2001)77, May 29, 2001, paragraph 43.

[2] See *Presidency Report to the Göteborg European Council on European Security and Defence Policy*, Brussels, June 11, 2001, paragraph 32. This method was a device to get around the Turkish hold on reaching formal decisions at NATO. Notably, the next sentence of this section on permanent arrangements was the following: "In the relations between the EU and NATO as organisations, there will be no discrimination against any of the Member States."

[3] See *NATO Update*, February 5–11, 2001, www.nato.int/docu/update/2001/0205/index-e.htm. The EU Council agreed on January 22 to the NATO proposal for holding consultation meetings. See Thomas Skold, "Center for European Security and Disarmament," *NATO Notes*, Brussels, Vol. 3, No. 1, January 30, 2001, p. 3:

first ambassadors' meeting in February was about process; but part was also about policy—the situation in the Western Balkans—thus crossing a watershed in relations between the two institutions and showing that something was possible beyond "theology."[4] Indeed, in practice, the Balkans issue has already provided a spur to institutional cooperation between the EU and NATO, as Bosnia proved to be a spur for NATO's transformation and political resurgence a half-decade earlier—although it is still not clear whether the current experience will set a lasting precedent for development of the overall NATO-EU/ESDP relationship.[5]

During the spring of 2001, NATO and the EU sought to find ways of resolving the key outstanding issues, although they were handicapped in part by the hold placed by Turkey on reaching final agreements. During this period, Britain was most active in trying to broker compromises.[6] This was especially true with regard to the role to be played in ESDP processes by non-EU NATO members. For example, it was agreed informally that the EU contributors committee, noted earlier, would work by consensus, and the EU's Political and Security Committee would normally rely on what the contributors committee decided when the interests of any non-EU NATO member was involved; there would be no operations without this

---

[There will also] . . . be continuous flow of meetings and information exchange in a plethora of meeting formats such as between the organizations' Secretaries-General, Secretariats, Military Committees, Military Staffs, and various *ad hoc* and expert working groups as needed. Further, high-level officials from each organization will attend meetings of the other as needed. The organizations can request additional meetings as necessary, and in times of crisis the contacts and the meetings will be stepped up.

[4]*NATO Update,* February 5–11, 2001, op. cit.:

Regarding NATO-EU relations, Ambassadors discussed ongoing business between the two organisations and the elements that remain to be resolved; regarding the situation in the [sic] Bosnia and Herzegovina and Kosovo, they voiced their concern over ongoing violence in the region and stated that NATO and the EU are working together to help stabilise the situation.

[5]*Presidency Report to the Göteborg European Council on European Security and Defence Policy,* June 11, 2001, op. cit., paragraph 33.

[6]Materials here and in the following two paragraphs are based on the author's interviews with senior EU and NATO officials in Brussels, June 2001.

consensus. However, final agreement foundered just before the May foreign ministers' meeting of the North Atlantic Council.[7]

Furthermore, although agreement between NATO and the EU on "permanent arrangements" was not yet possible, the January 2001 NATO-Sweden exchange of letters provided significant latitude for common effort, even though both Turkey and Norway sought greater assurances about their role in the ESDP consultative process and continued to have doubts whether arrangements were adequate for their participation in EU activities under ESDP. At the same time, NATO and the EU came close to completing work on a security agreement (on protecting information, etc.);[8] but "Berlin-plus" discussions continued at a slow pace. A key element has been determining the role to be played within ESDP by Allied Command Europe's Deputy Supreme Allied Commander and how he would be selected.[9]

The most critical issues discussed during this period related to ESDP planning. On defense planning, NATO Assistant Secretary General for Defence Planning and Operations Edgar Buckley reportedly tried to break a major impasse by brokering an informal agreement on the way in which a three-part process would work. The three parts are (1) an EU internal review mechanism, as decided by the European Council at Nice;[10] (2) adaptation of the NATO defense planning sys-

---

[7]Reportedly, the deal was rejected by the Turkish military (not enough conceded by the EU) and also Greek representation at the EU (too much conceded). Ibid.

[8]At the Budapest foreign ministers' meeting of the North Atlantic Council on May 29, the ministers noted

the successful implementation of the NATO-EU interim agreement on the security of information established last year and welcome[d] the progress made in preparing a permanent security agreement between the two organisations, including the productive work in the NATO-EU Ad Hoc Working Group on Security Issues. [They reiterated their] readiness to conclude a permanent security agreement between NATO and the EU as a matter of priority (Ministerial Meeting of the North Atlantic Council, May 29, 2001, op. cit., paragraph 44).

[9]Ibid. One suggestion for selecting Deputy SACEUR would preserve NATO's formal authority for making the appointment but would also provide for consultations first with the European Union.

[10]Nice European Council, *Presidency Conclusions,* December 7–9, 2000, "Annex VI: Presidency Report on the European Security and Defence Policy," op. cit., paragraph VIII:

tem; and (3) some relationship between the two. The difficult part is to agree on the third element. One important proposal in this context is to work toward a common Defense Planning Questionnaire (DPQ), beginning with at least a common data base.[11] With regard to operational planning, the evolution of understanding was that the EU was unlikely to conduct any of its own—that it would not attempt to duplicate NATO's capabilities—but rather would rely upon those capabilities, provided "assured access" were formally agreed upon, which was a provision of "Berlin-plus." However, as earlier described in EU *Presidency Conclusions* at the Nice summit, there could still be circumstances, regarding military operations on the Petersberg list, where national planning capabilities could be used.[12] In practice, that would mean Britain or France, but there was general understanding that all operational planning would be fully transparent to NATO and the EU.[13]

At the May 29 Budapest meeting of NATO foreign ministers, the NATO allies formally recognized what had been achieved, in both formal and informal efforts with the EU to sort out remaining issues. It was notable—but not accidental—that progress was assisted by the two institutions' cooperation over the Macedonia crisis, and especially the joint diplomatic missions of Lord Robertson and Javier

---

6. In order to ensure continuing European action to strengthen capabilities, the Member States agreed on the importance of defining an evaluation mechanism enabling follow-up and progress towards the realisation of the commitments made with a view to achieving the headline goal, in both quantitative and qualitative terms.

See this reference for details of the mechanism.

[11]These were comments to the author by a senior NATO official. By mid-year, there were reports that the idea of a common DPQ could be acceptable to France, which since the 1960s had not taken part in this process linked to the NATO integrated military structure. Having all countries engaged in European security, whether in NATO or in the EU, following a consistent defense planning process, is important in gaining a clear understanding of what various national forces can do, in promoting interoperability, and in identifying shortfalls as measured against a common understanding of what military forces might be called upon to do.

[12]Ibid.

[13]Author's notes on comments by French defense minister Alain Richard, Center for Strategic and International Studies, Washington, D.C., July 9, 2001.

Solana.[14] At Budapest, NATO emphasized several issues: the importance of strengthened European military capabilities, for both "the
Alliance's missions and . . . EU-led operations for Petersberg tasks
where the Alliance as a whole is not engaged";[15] the value of non-EU
European allied forces for EU-led operations; bilateral meetings the
EU had been holding with these allies "to clarify and evaluate their
contributions to European crisis management *on the basis of the
same criteria as those applying to EU member states* [emphasis
added]"; the EU's recognition of the need to improve capabilities; the
mutually reinforcing nature of the NATO DCI and the EU's Headline
Goal; and consultations taking place through a group called "HTF
Plus" (i.e., the EU states and NATO participants).[16]

---

[14]Ministerial Meeting of the North Atlantic Council, May 29, 2001, op. cit., paragraphs
28 and 41:

> We particularly welcome the close cooperation between NATO and the EU,
> as exemplified by the joint missions to Skopje by the NATO Secretary
> General and the EU High Representative. . . . The close consultation and co-
> operation between the two organisations and the mutually reinforcing steps
> taken by them in responding to the situation in the Balkans show that NATO
> and the EU have engaged in successful practical cooperation on questions of
> common interest relating to security, defence and crisis management.
> Continuing such practical cooperation between the two organisations will
> help ensure that crises can be met with the most appropriate military re-
> sponse and effective crisis management ensured.

[15]Ibid., paragraph 45:

> The European Allies are committed to further strengthening their military
> capabilities and to reinforcing the Alliance's European pillar. This will
> enhance their ability to contribute both to the Alliances' missions and to
> EU-led operations for Petersberg tasks where the Alliance as a whole is not
> engaged. We note that this process does not imply the creation of a
> European army and that the commitment of national resources for EU-led
> operations will be based on sovereign decisions.

[16]Ibid., paragraph 46:

> The significant additional contributions offered by non-EU European Allies
> to the pool of forces available for EU-led operations are important and will
> enhance the range of capabilities potentially available to the EU. We wel-
> come the bilateral meetings held between the EU and the non-EU European
> Allies in order to clarify and evaluate their contributions to European crisis
> management on the basis of the same criteria as those applying to EU mem-
> ber states and look forward to the further development of this practice. We
> note the EU's recognition of the need for further capability improvements.
> The Alliance's Defence Capabilities Initiative is also supporting the en-
> hancement of European capabilities. The objectives arising from NATO's
> DCI and the EU's Headline Goal are mutually reinforcing. We note with sat-

The NATO ministers zeroed in on one issue: "the importance of finding solutions satisfactory to all Allies [regarding] the issue of participation [in ESDP activities]."[17] They stressed a number of areas in which there had been significant progress—and not just regarding the concerns of Turkey (and to a lesser degree of Norway), by making a special reference to "progress made in developing dialogue, cooperation and consultation between Canada and the EU."[18] Indeed, the ministers again stressed that the alliance "is proceeding on the principle that nothing will be agreed until everything is agreed—the participation issue is also relevant in this context"; but they held out promise that critical issues remaining could be resolved, which could be characterized as "Berlin-double-plus": EU assured access to NATO operational planning; presumed availability of NATO assets; identification of EU command options, including "developing the role of DSACEUR in order for him to assume fully and effectively his European responsibilities"; and adaptation of NATO defence plan-

---

isfaction that NATO, upon request by the EU Presidency and on the basis of a Council decision, agreed to support for the duration of the Swedish EU Presidency the work of the HTF Plus through a team of experts open to national experts of those Allies who wish to participate in this work. In order to continue this important work during the next EU Presidency, NATO stands ready to provide, subject to an early Council decision, further expert advice upon request by the EU.

This convoluted reference to the HTF Plus reflected Turkey's resistance to having such cooperation between NATO and the EU on a *carte blanche* basis.

[17]Ibid., paragraph 47:

We continue to underline . . . the importance of finding solutions satisfactory to all Allies to the issue of participation. . . . Allies look forward to further broad and effective practical implementation of the arrangements agreed by the European Council at Nice for dialogue, consultation and cooperation with non-EU European Allies on issues related to security and defence policy and crisis management as well as the modalities for participation in EU-led military operations. We welcome the EU's commitment to intensify consultation in times of crisis. . . . Consultation and cooperation are particularly important with the EU Political and Security Committee and the EU Military Committee and, as appropriate, with the EU military staff, so as to ensure that the Allies concerned derive maximum benefit from them and to enable the Allies concerned to contribute effectively.

[18]Ibid., paragraph 48: "This includes a joint commitment to intensify consultation in times of crisis, particularly when the EU is considering an operation using NATO assets and capabilities."

ning.[19] These four items plus "participation" thus seemed to constitute the agenda for a final NATO-EU bargain.

The narrowing of the set of *institutional* concerns also reflected the
reality of the two bodies' memberships—that fully 11 members of the
EU are also NATO allies and that nothing could find its way into a
NATO communiqué unless it has the blessing of these 11, including
France, the most ambitious for ESDP among EU members. This illustrates the value of membership overlap, consultations among, and
even within governments; the pressures to reach agreement within
the EU and formal consensus within NATO; and mutual understanding that the United States—as "chief stakeholder" in NATO—must
have its own concerns about ESDP taken fully into account. By May
2001, therefore, it was becoming clear that a new process of interaction between NATO and the EU had been created and that, by and
large, it was starting to work.

What was, in effect, the EU response came at the Göteborg European
Council meeting of June 15–16, the days immediately following the
summit with President George W. Bush. Especially important was a
voluminous *Presidency Report* on ESDP, reflecting considerable detailed efforts. The EU thus had significant work to report, including
in the important area of civilian aspects of crisis management;[20] the

---

[19]Ibid., paragraph 49:

> Intensified discussions on the participation issue since our last meeting in
> December have strengthened the prospects for progress on the various as-
> pects of the Washington [summit] agenda and specifically on arrangements
> for:

- assured EU access to NATO planning capabilities able to contribute to
  military planning for EU-led operations;

- the presumption of availability to the EU of pre-identified NATO capabilities and common assets for use in EU-led operations;

- the identification of a range of European command options for EU-led
  operations, further developing the role of Deputy SACEUR in order for
  him to assume fully and effectively his European responsibilities; and

- the further adaptation of the Alliance's defence planning system.

[20]This has been a major focus of the overall EU effort with regard to ESDP. Particularly
important has been the development of a police capacity, building on decisions made
at the Feira European Council. This has been a notable problem with the conduct of

creation of "permanent political and military structures" in the council and its secretariat;[21] and progress in building "a permanent and effective relationship with NATO . . . agreed and implemented, as exemplified by the close cooperation in crisis management in the Western Balkans."[22] The EU also reported that

> Arrangements have been implemented concerning the consultation and participation of non-European NATO members and other

---

both SFOR and KFOR, and the EU effort can fill in a major gap in necessary capabilities for peacekeeping. See Ibid., "Annex I: Police Action Plan" and "Annex II: Contributions of Non-EU States to EU Police Missions in Civilian Crisis Management." Also see ibid., "Annex III: New Concrete Targets for Civilian Aspects of Crisis Management" and "Annex V: EU Co-operation with International Organisations in Civilian Aspects of Crisis Management."

[21]Interim ESDP bodies had been made permanent:

- The PSC, which became permanent on 22 January 2001, deals with all CFSP issues, including ESDP. The establishment of the PSC has strengthened the ability of the Union to deal with these issues and to address crisis situations in a coherent way.

- The EU Military Committee became permanent on 9 April, when the Council appointed the permanent chairman of the EUMC [General Gustav Hägglund, retiring Finnish Chief of Defence]. The EUMC is responsible for providing the PSC with military advice and recommendations on all military matters within the EU as well as providing military direction to the EUMS.

- The EU Military Staff was declared permanent on 11 June [under German Lieutenant General Rainer Schuwirth]. The EUMS, under the military direction of the EUMC, provides military expertise and support to the ESDP, including the conduct of EU-led military crisis management operations (*Presidency Report to the Göteborg European Council on European Security and Defence Policy*, June 11, 2001, op. cit., paragraph 20).

The council adopted a Regulation for a Rapid Reaction Mechanism in February 2001 (ibid., paragraph 24). . . . Work has been carried out which should enable the Council to take decisions in the near future, to establish as agencies a European Union Satellite Centre and a European Union Institute for Security Studies in support of the CFSP, including the ESDP (ibid., paragraph 25).

[22]Ibid., paragraph 40. This sentence was followed by: "Rapid agreement is called for on arrangements permitting EU access to NATO assets and capabilities."

countries which are candidates for access to the EU, and relations with Canada.[23]

The special notation of Canada—as in the communiqué of the NATO foreign ministers' meeting two weeks earlier—could have derived from the strong concerns that its defense minister, in particular, has expressed about Canada's being sidelined by ESDP preparations.[24]

In addition, the Göteborg European Council took steps to promote ESDP's military capabilities. Reaffirming that by 2003 the EU would

---

[23]Ibid., paragraph 50. It is interesting that, in considering "consultation and participation of non-EU European NATO members," the summit elaborated on the overall EU relationship with Turkey:

> Good progress has been made in implementing the pre-accession strategy for Turkey. . . . However, in a number of areas such as human rights, further progress is needed. Turkey is urged to take concrete measures to implement the priorities of the Accession Partnership (ibid., paragraph 10).

[24]*Presidency Report to the Göteborg European Council on European Security and Defence Policy,* June 11, 2001, op. cit., paragraph 45.

> Canada, with its long experience in peacekeeping, is a valuable partner to the European Union in the area of the ESDP. The EU welcomes the readiness of Canada to contribute to crisis management efforts undertaken by the Union. . . . [T]he EU and Canada have begun regular consultations on ESDP-related issues of mutual concerns. The EU will work with Canada to take forward the modalities for Canadian participation in EU-led operations.

See Hon. Art Eggleton, Minister of National Defence, "Transatlantic Relations and European Security and Defence Identity," Munich, Germany, February 3, 2001:

> We—like some other Allies—have concerns about the direction the NATO-EU relationship might go. First, EU structures for crisis management operations should strengthen, not detract from, NATO's role as the primary body for addressing Euro-Atlantic security challenges. In short, Canada would have serious difficulties with anything that weakened NATO's current consultative practices and consensus-based decision-making. . . . [W]e need to have appropriate arrangements for situations where the EU would expect to use NATO's assets and capabilities. . . . We need assurances that we would be involved in any decision on the role and manner of deployment of these forces [NATO assets]. . . . While the EU has welcomed the possibility of Canadian participation, we have yet to agree on the modalities. . . . A central issue for us is that, in any EU-led operations, we have adequate access to decision-making on matters affecting the deployment of Canadian forces. . . . [T]o be excluded from the strategic planning at the earliest stage would be politically unacceptable. And, I suspect, equally unacceptable to other non-EU Allies. If ESDI fails to respond to these fundamental political realities, grave problems await us.

be able "to deploy rapidly and then sustain forces capable of the full range of Petersberg tasks, *including the most demanding* [emphasis added],"[25] the council approved an EU exercise policy and an EU exercise programme. "The Exercise Policy identifies the EU requirements for and categories of exercises, including joint exercises with NATO," from 2001–2006.[26] Furthermore, working with the forthcoming Belgian EU presidency, the Swedish presidency

> has developed a plan for the work on military capabilities in order to ensure the appropriate preparation of a Capability Improvement Conference in November 2001 . . . [at which] Member States will be asked to commit themselves to specific additional measures in order to address the identified shortfalls.[27]

The object of all these activities was to point to the December 2001 European Council at Laeken, under the Belgian presidency, as the moment of decision for "achieving the objective of making the EU [i.e., ESDP] quickly operational"[28]—in other words, "the operational capacity of the EU crisis management organs."[29] Remarkably, during the first half of 2001, the EU both drove decisively forward with at least the bureaucratic aspects of creating ESDP and showed considerable sensitivity to concerns expressed by the United States and by other non-EU members of NATO. As was evident at the preceding meeting of NATO foreign ministers, the process within the EU was also working, and the prospects for productive agreement between the two bodies were steadily rising. Work remains to be done—as both admit—but the estrangement of "two institutions

---

[25]*Presidency Report to the Göteborg European Council on European Security and Defence Policy,* June 11, 2001, op. cit., paragraph 8.

[26]Ibid., paragraph 27. See also "Annex IV: Exercise Policy of the European Union."

[27]*Presidency Report to the Göteborg European Council on European Security and Defence Policy,* June 11, 2001, op. cit., paragraph 11.

[28]Göteborg European Council, *Presidency Conclusions,* June 15, 2001, op. cit., paragraph 51.

[29]Speech by Alain Richard, May 17, 2001, op. cit.:

> This year we will achieve the operational capacity of the EU crises [sic] management organs, which are professional, decisive and consistent with the preservation of the full sovereignty of governments; and we will reach a new step in enhancing and improving the effective collective capabilities we have decided to develop.

living in the same city as though on different planets" seems to be gradually giving way in the face of practical efforts.

Chapter Eighteen

STRIKING THE BALANCE: A U.S. VIEW

From 1993—when the United States first indicated that it would be truly open to a vigorous "European pillar" within the alliance, through the Berlin-Brussels agreements of 1996 and the "Berlin-plus" agreement of 1999, to the building of major bureaucratic structures for a European Security and Defense Policy—much has happened, not just in this one corner of the development of transatlantic relations for the 21st century, but in the total corpus of European security. NATO has admitted three new members and promises to take in more—its "open door"—at the November 2002 Prague NATO summit. The European Union is also moving deliberately toward expanding its membership. Both institutions are deeply engaged in Central Europe, in Russia, and in the Balkans. And both are "deepening": the European Union more obviously, with its European Monetary Union; with its Single European Currency, the Euro, in early 2002 to replace 12 national currencies; and with its efforts to leap ahead with a now-fledgling but to-be-fully-developed Common Foreign and Security Policy and European Security and Defense Policy—in some senses final acts of the devolution of sovereignty and thus still a long time in developing, but clearly now on the way.

For its part, NATO has also been "deepening," in that it has reaffirmed the United States' role as a permanent European power; preserved and modernized its critical integrated military command structures; engaged a wide variety of other states in its unique Partnership for Peace (and companion Euro-Atlantic Partnership Council); begun efforts to forge a potential "strategic partnership" with Russia and a "special partnership" with Ukraine; revamped its military strategy and commands (including its innovative Combined

Joint Task Force headquarters); and, for the first time, engaged twice in actual combat and in two post-conflict peacekeeping forces—all with intense lessons for the future of European security and NATO's role in helping to create a "Europe whole and free."

Within this overarching framework for building European security for the future (in which other institutions—such as the UN, the Organization for Security and Cooperation in Europe [OSCE], and the Council of Europe—also play roles), special attention is now being paid to the European Security and Defense Identity, or Policy—successor to the Western European Union—and to its relationship with NATO. As ESDP has developed, at least 11 separate purposes have emerged as central:

- Move forward the process of European integration.

- Lay the basis for, one day, having a truly functioning "European" foreign policy—potentially with concomitant engagements and responsibilities beyond the continent of Europe, including in response to requests from the United Nations.

- Provide one framework for adjusting relative political influence within the European Union (in this case centering primarily on France and its relations with other states, especially Germany).[1]

- Enable the Europeans to have an added insurance policy—however minor it may prove to be—that they could act with military force in some limited circumstances if, for some reason, NATO (meaning, in practice, the United States) chose not to be engaged; realistically, this would be most likely to apply in some areas beyond Europe, such as parts of Africa—assuming, of course, that the European members of ESDP were inclined to take military action, either within the Petersberg Tasks or as an extension of them.

----

[1]As an added benefit for France, the creation of a Headline Goal Task Force that could—and would—take action in the event of military contingencies in francophone Africa would help reduce the burdens on Paris' acting alone. This could be part of Paris' attempt to exert added influence in Europe in the foreign policy and security realm. In theory, of course, other European countries could seek to use the rapid reaction force, or just EU crisis-management capabilities, in outside-of-Europe situations where they have unique or at least preeminent interests.

- Do something to address the constant refrain from the United States about burden sharing within the alliance, among other things to reinforce U.S. incentives to remain engaged with Europe's strategic and political future, while also giving the Europeans some more weight in deciding, politically, where NATO should be involved militarily, and how.

- Provide some added political incentive for modernizing indigenous military forces, especially difficult in the absence of a palpable military threat—modernization that can also help European militaries remain, to the degree possible, interoperable with more-rapidly modernizing U.S. military forces.

- Give the Europeans, through the European Union, some more say in decisions reached within NATO—an incentive reinforced after the Kosovo conflict, even though that conflict in fact also reinforced the sense that NATO would be required—for the indefinite future—to undertake any military operation of that size and complexity and with comparable political constraints.

- Buttress the process of EU enlargement into Central Europe, while also helping to give those European allies concerned a sense of being able to compete for influence there with the United States.

- Spur the consolidation of European armaments industries, both within and across borders, provide some added demand for their goods and services, and create a political framework for both competing and cooperating with their American counterparts.

- Tackle the long-standing question of the relative distribution of influence between the United States and its European partners within the broader Atlantic Alliance: an inchoate aspiration, but one that is behind much of the debate—on both sides of the Atlantic—about the future of ESDP and its relationship to NATO.

- Give European governments a greater say—and reduce pressure on them—regarding a legal mandate for military action. This was an important issue at the time of the Kosovo conflict: where NATO acted without a formal mandate either from the United Nations Security Council (UNSC) (under Chapter VII of the UN Charter) or OSCE, a situation that caused considerable difficulty for several governments. Thus, it is important that various EU documents on ESDP stress that it "recognizes the United Nations Security Council's primary responsibility for the maintenance of international peace and security."[2]

For the United States, there is much to welcome in most if not all of these ESDP goals. The United States has long supported European integration, not as an end in itself, but among other things as a proven method of reducing the risks of future conflict in Europe and now as a means of increasing a sense of security in Central Europe. The U.S. desire for an increased European role in defense, both relatively and absolutely (and adjusted for post–cold war conditions), has a long pedigree but also a long record of mutual frustration on the two sides of the Atlantic. The United States clearly welcomes efforts that will reduce recurrent European fears, much diminished since the end of the cold war, that somehow the United States will "decouple" its security from Europe's. It welcomes incentives to increase—or at least stabilize—European defense spending, especially where this will help the European militaries to be interoperable with NATO forces and, specifically, to be consistent with the alliance's Defense Capabilities Initiative.

The United States should welcome the development of a Headline Goal Task Force that focuses on development of military capabilities, especially in peacemaking and peacekeeping, and whose military capabilities in the main can also contribute to NATO operations—given that most of the basic European forces would be virtually the same, whether employed by NATO or by the European Union under ESDP.

Furthermore, the United States should welcome development of a CFSP and ESDP that can, in time, lead the European nations to play a more active role beyond Europe—assuming, of course, that the respective strategic visions of the United States and, in general, the European allies will be compatible if not identical (since they are not, at times—notably in places like the zone of Arab-Israeli conflict). In areas where the United States would have significant interests, this

---

[2]Göteborg European Council, *Presidency Conclusions,* June 15, 2001, op. cit., paragraph 47. Of course, even NATO relates to the UNSC's "primary responsibility." In these ESDP documents, however, the reference can be read to have more-than-routine political significance.

European capacity to act beyond the continent would also assume that the United States would be prepared to share assessment of threats and challenges beyond Europe, what should be done about them and by whom, and the process of decision and control regarding foreign policies and, potentially, military action. By contrast, where the United States did *not* have significant interests, or were content to see the Europeans simply act on their own—and this applies to much of Africa, both parts of the Maghreb and much of sub-Saharan Africa—then European efforts should be seen by the United States as clearly positive, so long as there were no distraction from a simultaneous need for the use of European military assets in a crisis affecting NATO.[3] Also—as a quality often discussed but not so often emphasized—the United States should welcome a European capability for crisis management, especially civilian aspects, and even the use of military force that falls below the threshold where NATO would need (or want) to become engaged, but which nonetheless can be effective—operation Alba, to help stabilize Albania in April 1997, readily comes to mind.[4] And there can be significant benefits from "European capacity for action in the civil fields," that would not have to be duplicated by NATO—or the United States;[5] indeed, the EU has some unique advantages in dealing with situations in a holistic way—including political, civilian, nongovernmental organization, and economic instruments—that NATO cannot match.

---

[3] As the French defense minister said in February 2001,

> the European capacity that we are establishing will widen the range of tools available to the transatlantic community for crisis management. Our American allies must be able to decide on their participation in the management of a crisis without being constrained by European impotence to endorse alone the choice between action or abstention (Alain Richard, February 3, 2001, op. cit.).

[4] Of course, this operation was led by Italy, after the WEU turned it down—among other reasons, because Germany did not want to engage in a second operation when it was testing the limits of its political ability to use military force (in the Bosnia Stabilization Force) and because the United Kingdom was at best ambivalent about the WEU's undertaking a military operation on its own.

[5] See Alain Richard, February 3, 2001, op. cit. Also:

> The development of a European crisis-management capacity, which has become necessary for Europe if it is to assume its responsibilities, is therefore useful to the Alliance, and strengthens our transatlantic partnership (ibid.).

These are all on the positive side of the ledger. But there are also negatives for the United States to be found in the European Security and Defense Policy (and aspects of CFSP, as well). Most of these negatives are about method, however, rather than about purpose and intent. These issues will need to be resolved in order to ensure that NATO and EU/ESDP will be compatible with one another, that they will work toward the same basic objectives, and that transatlantic security and political relations will be strengthened, not weakened, by the development of ESDP. The key problems for the United States so far identified center on the following:

- ESDP may stimulate some greater European defense spending, but that spending might go primarily to purchase capabilities that NATO already has in abundance; or it could be wasteful in terms of efficient use of scarce resources (e.g., the A400M large transport aircraft and even the Eurofighter); or it could stimulate (for political reasons) European efforts to close or restrict arms markets to competition from outside, including the United States. "Unnecessary duplication" is more than just a U.S. slogan; it risks becoming a serious reality. Likewise, candidates for NATO membership could be pressed to accede to ESDP requirements (including "buying European") at the expense of preparing to be effective NATO allies.

- By contrast, ESDP could, in time, lead some allies to believe that they can meet the military requirements of the Headline Goal Task Force—and thus domestic political requirements—without facing the much more onerous and expensive demands of NATO force modernization, especially the DCI, at a time of rapid U.S. modernization, thereby risking the "hollowing out" of alliance military capabilities. In other words, the "talk" of ESDP and its institutions could substitute for the "walk" of increased defense capabilities.

- The elaboration of structures and processes in ESDP could, whether intended or not, cause competition with NATO's structures and processes, if only because "the beast has to be fed": structures once in being get used and, at a certain level of bureaucratic size and complexity (the EUMS is already significant in both size and competence), can compete successfully for the attention and priority required to keep NATO processes as effective as possible. Indeed, an ESDP as political and bureaucratic distraction from NATO may become the chief legitimate U.S. worry.

- Also, the still not-entirely-resolved differences regarding planning (not limited to Turkey's circumstances) have special significance for NATO. First, having more than one place where operational planning takes place could potentially lead to differences in outcomes that could, at the very least, complicate any situation in which the EU, acting on the basis of ESDP, had to hand over responsibility to NATO, or where NATO had to decide what forces it could usefully transfer to an ESDP operation without prejudicing its own ability to act—a cardinal point from the June 1996 Brussels agreement. The problem would be greater if there were not total transparency in the planning processes—which in fact can only be assured if NATO's planning staff is constantly in the same room with ESDP's—e.g., a national planning staff—and if ESDP planners are at NATO.[6] Among other things, any translation (escalation) of a crisis from one conducted by the European Union through ESDP to one conducted by NATO—whether non-Article 5 or Article 5—could become that much more difficult and potentially dangerous. There have been indications that this problem could be resolved by maintaining the locus of planning in the main within NATO, assuming that Turkey's objections to completing the process of NATO-ESDP relations were lifted.[7] This compromise could still leave "national" headquarters (in practice, either Britain or France) acting on only some relatively low-level operations or on military operations in some specific areas (such as parts of Africa) where there would be a low probability of NATO engagement but a possibility that European states would want to act. This might prove an effective compromise; but the point about NATO in a fully transparent en-

---

[6]As late as February 2001, the French defense minister said that:

> Where an operation does not call on NATO assets, an operational staff formed around a core provided by a national strategic staff will carry out the operational planning. This staff would be multinational and reinforced by officers from the other nations participating in the operation (Alain Richard, February 3, 2001, op. cit.).

[7]Comments to the author by various EU and NATO officials, Brussels, May–June 2001.

gagement with ESDP operational planning, wherever conducted, is still important, both in principle and in practice.

Second, if defense planning—i.e., developing force structures over time—were bifurcated, with NATO's adopting one system and ESDP's adopting another, inconsistencies, incompatibilities, and inefficiencies—already the bane of military planners in the alliance—could become worse. Bifurcation of course would make more difficult the process of relating ESDP activities to those of NATO, could complicate the problem of interoperability, could put decisions directed toward developing the Headline Goal Task Force at variance with NATO requirements, and could introduce uncertainties regarding the potential transition from an EU/ESDP to a NATO operation. To be sure, most of the current EU states take part in NATO's procedures, including the critical Defense Planning Questionnaire; but not all do. Important will be whether France agrees to adopt (or mimic) the DPQ, and whether the two defense planning processes are both sufficiently compatible with, and transparent to, one another. Even so, with both operational and defense planning, the development of any competing ESDP capabilities would make NATO's life more trying.

- Additionally, the demands of internal political cohesion within the EU could make it difficult to resolve the issue of full participation by non-EU NATO members—notably Turkey—as a matter of EU process integrity (if not theology), thus risking a split in the invaluable, if not indispensable, sense of cohesion among allied states, without gaining anything truly significant in return (i.e., a rapid reaction force that would in fact be undertaking major responsibilities for European security). Of course, Turkey risks exaggerating the problems that lie in the way of its effective engagement with ESDP; it may be using these issues as part of its more important political concerns about membership in the EU; and its actions—at least as evident through mid-2001—could cause it to lose the moment, in terms of NATO's having as much influence as possible on the shaping of ESDP practices and procedures. But Turkey's concerns are not without merit, and if these concerns are not reasonably satisfied (along with those, in particular, of Norway and Canada), a shadow would be cast over other NATO–EU/ESDP relations.

- The political impetus to make CFSP and ESDP effective could lead not only to an "integrity" in the relationship between crisis management and employment of force that NATO cannot currently match for reasons noted above (this is NATO's problem), but also to support for full implementation of the Maastricht and Amsterdam provisions for coordination of national positions in international institutions—in effect, a "European caucus" within NATO that, if truly pursued to meet the provisions of the Consolidated Version of the Treaty on European Union, could impair the capabilities of the North Atlantic Council and could tend to produce "least common denominator" outcomes. Here, pragmatic solutions might be effective, and it is true that, in all countries that belong to both NATO and the EU, there are "internal consultations"; but even if the EU states pay mere lip-service to the Maastricht and Amsterdam provisions, lack of clarity about the process can reduce confidence, especially in Washington.

- Also, the process of relating crisis management to the use of force—where CFSP/ESDP operates quite differently from NATO and whatever body or country assumes responsibility, on a case-by-case basis, for NATO-related political crisis management—could complicate the issue of determining just how NATO would gain what the United States sees, but not all European allies see, as a necessary right of first refusal—i.e., when it would be determined that NATO as a whole is not prepared to be engaged. This could become a significant problem, especially if one or more European countries were bent upon trying, perhaps for political reasons, to manage a crisis and an accompanying military action without recourse to NATO—however illogical that proposition would be given the value of using the full range of NATO capabilities, including the spreading of political risk to include the United States, whenever possible.[8]

---

[8]The possibility of tactical differences among even the closest allies cannot be ruled out. Some instances include disagreements over peace plans for Bosnia in the early 1990s; differences over enforcement of the arms embargo against parties to that conflict; the complex way in which Operation Alba had to be put together to help Albania when neither NATO or the WEU were willing to act directly; and frequent squabbling, especially at the military level, over the conduct of the Kosovo campaign.

On the negative side of the ledger for the United States are some additional concerns, related to purpose and intent, of which the following are most important:

- European rhetoric about ESDP (and CFSP) could become so exaggerated—as is natural during a process of institution building—that some U.S. observers might (erroneously) believe that the EU/ESDP could take over more of the common burdens, and reduce those falling on U.S. shoulders, than would in fact be the case.

- Differences in the way in which the purposes of ESDP are characterized by different European states and political leaders could continue to sow confusion in the United States, especially about some instrumental relationships between NATO and EU/ESDP (e.g., on operational and defense planning), as well as about the types of operations the EU could actually undertake through ESDP. Such confusion could risk that EU/ESDP would be seen, in practice, as a potential competitor for NATO.

- A reverse problem could arise if a "division of labor" grew up between the European Union (ESDP) and NATO (especially along the lines of relatively high and low military technologies) however much both bodies recognize the problem inherent in a "division of risks"—e.g., airpower versus ground combat—and work to prevent it. This "division of labor" could produce an implicit fracture in the assumption that providing security in Europe is a common good to be pursued by all allies, although in practice in different ways depending on circumstances. Nor is this issue limited to the development of ESDP. The issue of whether the United States is prepared to share military tasks— and hence risks—with European allies has been a theme running through most debates about allied engagement in the Former Yugoslavia from the early 1990s onward. In Bosnia and Kosovo, these debates were eventually resolved, more or less successfully; but as of the time of this writing, it is not clear that such success will also hold true for Macedonia. Indeed, expressed U.S. doubts in 2001 about putting troops at risk in a NATO force for Macedonia raised some concern among other allies, with a significant impact on perceptions of the overall U.S. commitment to engage in real-life NATO activities containing some degree of risk. European perceptions on this general point have played a major role in the politics of ESDP's development.

There must be an important qualifier, however. There could emerge a "division of labor" in regard to crises or other challenges beyond Europe, in areas where the United States (perhaps with Canada and a few other allies) would not see its interests to be significantly engaged and where, therefore, the issue of NATO's becoming involved militarily might not arise and the allies might not require the United States to be engaged. This is especially true in parts of Africa. Indeed, had there been a European capacity for action (an effective rapid reaction force) in the 1990s, it is conceivable that Europeans might have decided to intervene in Rwanda, assuming that the added military capacities, a crisis-management mechanism, and a sense of "sharing the risk" would have produced more political will on the part of key states.[9] Left unaddressed, however, is another meaning of "division of labor": that the United States would want the allies to become engaged beyond Europe—truly "outside of area"—but would be unable to gain a consensus within the alliance to do so; this is the great "emperor has no clothes" of NATO's future.[10]

- Finally, the issue of the relative balance of influence between the United States and some or all European states could become sufficiently bound up with the structure and conduct of ESDP that crucial elements could be lost, such as the principles of common commitment by all allies to European security, risk

---

[9]See House of Lords, Select Committee on European Union, *Fifteenth Report,* July 25, 2000, paragraph 42:

> Surprisingly, a scenario like Rwanda was seen as particularly appropriate for EU involvement by Mr Richard Hatfield, Policy Director of the Ministry of Defence. He told us that "Were that situation to come up again, it could be done under European Union auspices but it would not be done under NATO auspices because NATO has no security role in relation to Central Africa.

Of course, the point is historically moot but interesting in terms of British Ministry of Defence thinking about the future of ESDP.

[10]Beyond the scope of this study are considerations of relying upon "permissive" decisions by the North Atlantic Council (NAC), but where only a few allies take part in military actions; the use of NATO infrastructure even where the NAC does not give its formal blessing—as happened during Operation Alba; or the development of "coalitions of the willing and able" to act with the United States "outside of area."

sharing, and subordination of such issues as the balance of political influence to more-practical matters of getting the European security job done.

Chapter Nineteen

PRACTICAL STEPS: BUILDING A TRANSATLANTIC BRIDGE—NOT A BARRIER

Even with these major qualifications, drawing the balance on ESDP for the United States produces a clear-cut answer. *The balance is strongly positive, provided that remaining problems—some of substance and process, some of perception—can be resolved effectively.*

"NATO FIRST"

There needs to be wholehearted, unambiguous European adherence to the principle of "where NATO as a whole is not engaged," and political processes should be developed to ensure that no doubts arise about this point or about NATO's ability, sufficiently early in a crisis, to make such a determination. Many Europeans will resist the notion that this implies "NATO first": But as a practical matter, it is important for preserving cohesion of the alliance. Securing this goal, which is important to the United States, will probably have to come from day-to-day consultations, including close cooperation between the North Atlantic Council, the EU's Political and Security Committee, and permanent, day-to-day liaison arrangements between the two; but it requires a shared vision and political commitment on all sides.

SHARED RISKS/NO DIVISION OF LABOR

At the same time, there needs to be reaffirmation—by all the allies, and at the moment especially by the United States—of the cardinal NATO principle that risks are to be shared by all allies; and that there must not emerge, formally or informally, a "division of labor" between NATO and the EU/ESDP or implicitly in regard to particular allies.[1] French Minister of Defense Alain Richard met this point head-on in a July 2001 speech in Washington:

> Does the development of a European reaction force create the very situation we want to avoid? Does it open the way for a division of labor with the United States taking care of the high end of the risk and conflict spectrum, and the Europeans focusing on the fire brigade function of local peace restoration in their vicinity? I believe such a division of labor, whether intended or accidental, would damage transatlantic relations and reduce our overall capacity to deter and manage new crises.[2]

Avoiding a division of labor is not just about what the EU nations do in regard to ESDP and, especially, both the structure and practical operation of the rapid reaction force and collective attitudes toward the Petersberg Tasks. Also critical is U.S. willingness (and, by implication, NATO's readiness) to be engaged in operations that fall below the threshold of "Article 5 operations" or what is sometimes called the "robust" end of the overall conflict spectrum. Specifically, U.S. reluctance to be engaged in future peacekeeping or peacemaking in Europe—operations such as those in Bosnia and Kosovo in recent years—could, in practice, tend to leave such tasks to EU/ESDP and

---

[1]As noted above, this applies to areas where interests of the United States and other allies are engaged, and where there could be collective military action appropriate to NATO. European-only actions in areas such as Africa would not pose a "division of labor" problem, so long as these actions did not conflict with simultaneous needs by NATO, lead to a shaping of European military forces that would not also be compatible with NATO requirements, or lead to a failure of full transparency of ESDP planning and operations.

[2]He continued:

> A key objective for this period of review we are going through is to avoid our going down separate specialized paths and to come out of this process with trans-Atlantic solidarity preserved and enhanced (*Security in the 21st Century—a European Perspective*, statement by Minister of Defense Alain Richard at the Center for Strategic and International Studies, Washington, D.C., July 9, 2001).

Of course, Richard's implication was also that the European rapid reaction force would be able to engage with the "high end of the risk and conflict spectrum"—a debatable point about its future potential—as opposed to seeing the common effort as focusing on NATO.

would, *per force,* lead to at least a perception of a division of labor—and of risk—within the alliance.

How the George W. Bush administration develops policies toward (a) the Balkans and (b) peacekeeping/peacemaking roles for U.S. forces, in general, cannot be separated from its hopes for an ESDP that is compatible with its hopes for NATO. In short, *U.S. reluctance to share such risks and tasks, especially in the Balkans, the most serious area of instability in today's Europe, would be incompatible with an effort to keep ESDP as simply a second-choice option for dealing with crisis and conflict in Europe.* Indeed, compared with ESDP developments, far more is at stake for the NATO Alliance from the Bush administration's reluctance in 2001 to be equally engaged with other allies in a NATO-led Macedonian military peace force.

COOPERATIVE PLANNING

Approaches to operational planning must not put NATO and EU/ESDP at loggerheads. In parallel, methods of defense planning must be mutually compatible (this point argues for a single set of processes, such as that proposed by former Defense Secretary Cohen). Cooperation should include shared contingency planning, conducted by the Combined Joint Planning Staff at Supreme Headquarters Allied Powers Europe (SHAPE), with full participation by the EUMS. In addition, simple military logic demands that there be only one methodology, for both NATO and EU/ESDP, regarding command, control, communications, and intelligence (C^3I). At the same time, the EU should sort out potential command arrangements before crises arise. It would inspire considerable confidence by pre-designating NATO's Deputy SACEUR as force generator, strategic coordinator, and operational commander for all ESDP missions.[3]

---

[3]By contrast, the French minister of defense has argued that

> In all probability this [operational commander] will be the Deputy SACEUR if the operation falls on NATO assets and capabilities, and a general officer from a member State when the operation does not use NATO assets (Alain Richard, February 3, 2001, op. cit.).

There would also be value in using Deputy SACEUR in the operational commander's role even for a military operation conducted beyond Europe, as in Africa; there, how-

DEFENSE SPENDING AND CAPABILITIES

European governments need to commit themselves to keep defense spending up or, where it is falling, to stop the slide (Germany is currently most important). Emphasis needs to be put on outputs, on capabilities relevant to well-analyzed future requirements, and on interoperability, not just as a matter of ESDP-NATO compatibility, but as a critical problem for the Atlantic Alliance as a whole. Even within existing budgets, efforts to promote the DCI must not slacken; however, by the time of the May 2001 NATO defense ministers' meeting in Brussels, the outlook was still less than bright.[4] At the very least, priorities within the DCI should emphasize core NATO requirements, extending to doctrine, training, and style of operations as well as to force structure and equipment. Allies should avoid duplicating NATO assets available to ESDP where these divert defense money away from other critical areas; the A400M transport aircraft is perhaps the most egregious current example of a misplaced use of scarce funds.[5] At the same time, if the United States wants ESDP to avoid "unnecessary duplication," it must find ways of reassuring the Europeans that NATO would, indeed, release NATO assets—the point of the language about "presumed access"—where this could include U.S. equipment operated by U.S. service members, especially large transport aircraft. From this perspective, the A400M would make sense only if there were circumstances—e.g., an African

---

ever, interests of a lead nation—most likely France, based on historical experience—could dictate otherwise for political as much as for military reasons.

[4]See North Atlantic Council, *Statement on the Defence Capabilities Initiative*, Meeting of the Defence Ministers Session, Brussels, NATO Press Release M-NAC-D-1 (2001)89, June 7, 2001:

> 2. Although progress has been made in certain areas, further efforts are required to achieve the necessary improvements. For example, a number of particularly critical and long-standing deficiencies exist in the areas of effective engagement and survivability of Alliance forces such as in the areas of suppression of enemy air defence and support jamming; combat identification; intelligence, surveillance and target acquisition (including the alliance Ground Surveillance system); air weapons systems for day/night and all weather operations; air defence in all its aspects, including against theatre ballistic missiles and cruise missiles; capabilities against nuclear, biological, and chemical (NBC) weapons and their means of delivery, and NBC detection and protection.

[5]Some Europeans would argue that the A400M will find major markets beyond Europe, thus becoming profitable in the long term.

ESDP operation—that would neither be of strategic interest to the United States nor where it would be willing to risk either aircraft or crews. The Europeans are right to expect clarity on this point. Of course, for the Europeans to buy some combination of U.S. C-130Js, C-17s, and Ukrainian AN-124s would still make better sense financially.[6]

INTEROPERABILITY

With this provision, the EU through ESDP needs to concentrate its force modernization on interoperability with NATO, especially within the DCI. This point and European defense spending are closely linked. It is critical, for example, that two levels of interoperability do not develop—one for the United States and a handful of key European allies (notably the U.K.), and one for the rest: This would be a sure recipe for bifurcation, an implicit if not explicit division of labor among alliance tasks—even worse if based in practice on differential risk-taking by high- versus relatively low-technology forces—and corrosion of the spirit of cohesion that has been a hallmark of the alliance. Furthermore, as noted above, interoperability is critical if the United States expects to be able to conduct out-of-Europe military operations with allies, either formally under NATO or as coalitions of the able and willing; here, in addition to shared responsibility to meet the goals of the DCI, the burden also rests on the United States, in terms of sharing high technology with allies, as a major priority. A "two-tier technology" alliance—certainly if there is not fully integrated C^3ISR—is not an alliance that can conduct serious outside-of-area operations; a CJTF headquarters can help, but it is unlikely to suffice.

---

[6]The issue whether the United States is prepared to share potential combat risks with allies in the Balkans has a direct bearing on this point: whether Washington would be willing to risk large transport aircraft—C-130Js, C-17s—and their aircrews in ESDP operations beyond Europe of minimal interest to the United States—i.e., where it could not be plausibly explained to the American people that this was a useful "division of labor" "outside of area."

NATO CRISIS MANAGEMENT

Meanwhile, NATO needs to develop means for being linked to a crisis management mechanism, paralleling the CFSP/ESDP relationship.[7] There must also be prior agreement that discussion and dialogue between NATO and the EU will be deep, wide, continuous, and effective at all stages of any emerging crisis that could conceivably affect both bodies. Of course, there is significant overlap between NATO and EU (ESDP) governments, which will consult both within their own bureaucracies and bilaterally with other governments. Furthermore, unless a crisis develops suddenly, there will likely be numerous informal exchanges between NATO and ESDP bodies. But relying on this method fails to provide clear lines of communication and authority, so that different parties will understand what to expect of one another in actual policies and behavior.[8] Where suspicion also exists—e.g., on Capitol Hill—about whether EU/ESDP is developing as NATO's competitor rather than complement, the question of when NATO becomes formally seized of a crisis could be significant. Even with NATO-ESDP cooperation over Macedonia in 2001, doubts about whether the United States would be willing to share risks with other allies in a peacekeeping force raised concerns about NATO's capacity to act as an effective crisis manager that could be relied upon to see matters through to the end.

---

[7]Notably, the EU also envisions a much more elaborate relationship with the United Nations than does NATO. It noted in June 2001:

> Substantial progress has been made in building an effective partnership with the UN in the fields of conflict prevention and crisis management as well as development cooperation, humanitarian affairs, asylum policies and refugee assistance. *This partnership is further strengthened by the mutually reinforcing approaches to conflict prevention and by ensuring that the European union's evolving military and civilian capacities provide real added value for UN crisis management activities* [emphasis added]. The Western Balkans, the Middle East and Africa will be given highest priority in this reinforced cooperation (Göteborg European Council, *Presidency Conclusions,* June 15, 2001, op. cit., paragraph 53).

[8]Of course, one common aspect of crises is that each one almost certainly contains some new and unpredictable elements that will call for responses going beyond any tried-and-true template.

POLITICAL FOCUS: EU/ESDP AND NATO

There is a premium on the rapid completion of basic ESDP and CFSP institution building—even though political maturation is still many years away—so that attention, both at the EU and, by default, at NATO, can begin moving from the current intense focus on developing bureaucratic structures related to ESDP and toward the what, the how, and the how much (in terms of real capabilities) of European security.

POLITICAL AND STRATEGIC DIALOGUES

There needs to be solid, sustained political and military dialogue at all levels—institutional, national, and personal—between ESDP/CFSP and NATO, and between individual national governments and parliaments. This is especially true regarding the U.S. Congress. These dialogues should also extend to the full range of complementary NATO and EU activities, including geography (e.g., Central Europe, Russia, Balkans) and function (e.g., NATO/EU enlargement and efforts like NATO's PFP [Partnership for Peace] and the EU's PHARE [Poland and Hungary Assistance for the Reconstruction of the Economy] and TACIS [Technical Assistance to the Commonwealth of Independent States] programs).

The transatlantic dialogue on burden sharing has often been poisoned by different definitions of the term: with the U.S. focus almost exclusively on military activity, and with the European demand for credit from nonmilitary contributions to a broader definition of "security." This difference of view is evident, today, in the Balkans. An open-minded, thoughtful, and intelligent dialogue on these issues across the Atlantic is essential if burden sharing (the analogue to risk sharing) is not to become an increasing irritant in transatlantic relations. Misjudged U.S. pressure on Europeans for burden sharing could translate, politically, not into added efforts to bolster NATO, but rather into incentives for increasing the role and influence of ESDP.

MANAGING RHETORIC AND AMBITION

The European Union needs to exercise restraint—and provide clarity—in its rhetoric about what ESDP is and what it is not, especially in dealing with the United States and even more particularly Congress. There is a risk that inflated declarations of ESDP aspirations will be taken for reality, where that is not justified, thus leading some Americans to believe that the United States can do less militarily in Europe than actual ESDP capabilities would warrant; alternatively, later shortfalls in ESDP, relative to declared aspirations, can intensify congressional criticisms that the Europeans are not pulling their weight. It is especially important that those members of the EU that most care about preserving the vitality and cohesion of the transatlantic relationship, as well as NATO's primacy, ensure that "autonomy" for European Union decision and action under ESDP not become the central focus of the European pillar; this aspiration needs to be kept in perspective in relation to other European security goals. A parallel risk is that some members of the U.S. Congress will read into excessive ESDP rhetoric more of a challenge to NATO's primacy—and to U.S. influence on the European continent—than any European leader really intends, thus deepening suspicions to no good effect. Preventing misperceptions, especially in Washington, requires EU discipline that is difficult to achieve in an institution made up of individual national governments that often have separate and somewhat different agendas and aspirations.

By the same token, the U.S. government needs to speak with as much of "one voice" as is possible for Washington. Certainly key officials should present U.S. support and aspirations for ESDP and concerns about its development clearly and consistently. President Bush's leadership on this issue needs to be followed throughout the bureaucracy. The administration also bears a major share of responsibility for ensuring that debates on Capitol Hill center on the facts of ESDP, not misperceptions about it.

DEFENSE-COOPERATION "CODE OF CONDUCT"

An effective transatlantic dialogue and a NATO-EU defense-cooperation code of conduct need to be developed for governments and industry. This code should focus on five principles: (1) make progress toward opening up to one another, or keeping open, U.S. and European arms markets; (2) share as much defense high technology within the alliance as possible; (3) develop common standards and measures for protecting shared technologies; (4) emphasize interoperability within transatlantic defense cooperation, for both NATO and EU/ESDP; and (5) at a minimum, within limited European defense budgets, focus on at least ensuring "open architecture"(the design of new technologies to permit compatibility with other allies' military equipment) to minimize the risks of a technologically two-tiered alliance. Furthermore, in time, there should be common NATO and ESDP acquisition planning to help harmonize requirements and responses.

USES OF MILITARY POWER

There needs to be a continuing, broad strategic dialogue within NATO about the purposes of military capabilities and defense spending. This last suggestion is in some ways the most difficult to implement, but in the long term it is perhaps the most important for NATO's future and for the EU's development of foreign policy and defense. For both NATO and EU/ESDP, building, training, sustaining, and exercising military forces must be clearly related to what they are actually expected, at some point, to do. (Both Bosnia and Kosovo helped NATO to find a sense of purpose—however limited and short run—when other purposes seemed very remote; Macedonia has proven in 2001 to be a test of how NATO and EU/ESDP, including crisis management and civilian operations, can work together.) These issues have long been put off—including at the Washington NATO summit, despite its adoption of a new Strategic Concept. But for democracies to continue spending significant funds on defense—and potentially to risk the lives of young men and women in military combat—strategic analysis, political vision, and dialogue among nations and institutions are indispensable.

LEADERSHIP

Finally, these recommendations for defusing possible disagreements within the alliance and across the Atlantic about ESDP need to be followed at the highest levels of government until key differences are resolved to the degree possible—that is, so that there is a productive, mutually reinforcing relationship between NATO and EU/ESDP, even if not always tension-free. Allied and EU leaders should focus on six key "cooperations" between NATO and the European Union: (1) operational planning, (2) contingency planning, (3) defense and capabilities planning, (4) acquisition planning and a transatlantic defense-cooperation code of conduct, (5) North Atlantic Council–Political and Security Committee interaction that ideally also engages the Euro-Atlantic Partnership Council, and (6) joint crisis management.

NATO-EU/ESDP relations must also be viewed in the perspective of other critical issues facing the alliance. "Getting ESDP right" is a necessary goal on its own; that, as argued here, should be able to be obtained with sufficient leadership, understanding, and commitment on both sides of the Atlantic. But that goal cannot be achieved in isolation. It is also essential for the allies to "get right" other critical, less-easily resolved, disagreements and differences of opinion on such matters as threats to allied territories from beyond Europe, missile defenses, defense investments by European allies, the risk of a "hollowed out" NATO, NATO enlargement, fostering development of PFP and the Euro-Atlantic Cooperation Council, engaging Russia, stability in the Balkans, and the long-term perspectives both of European security and of U.S. relations with Europe—not least, U.S. relations with the European Union in all dimensions.

Chapter Twenty

LOOKING TO THE FUTURE

As this study has sought to demonstrate, resolving current issues in NATO–EU/ESDP relations, including U.S. interests and concerns about the EU's ventures in foreign policy and defense, is, at least for the near and medium terms, more about political will and tactics than about long-term goals and strategy. At some point, the European Union is likely to have its own foreign policy—and, in some areas of economics-as-foreign-policy, it already does. Even beyond Europe, there continues to be a high degree of common strategic perspective among the United States, Canada, the European allies, the non-NATO members of the European Union, and the aspirants to join both organizations. But it is not clear precisely how much common strategic perspective there will be in the years ahead—in terms of what to do about emerging threats and challenges if not also about the nature of those threats and challenges themselves: The transatlantic debate on missile defenses—especially as it relates to the Middle East, Russia, China, and multilateral regimes (e.g., arms control)—is a case in point. Furthermore, as the European Union gains cohesion, economic coherence, and political potential—both within the European continent and beyond—questions of relative influence between Europe and the United States will grow apace. This trend will continue even if (as is likely) the strategic presence of the United States on the continent is still required, especially to help shape Russia's future, and even if the transatlantic economic relationship continues to move generally in the direction of interdependence (and motives for a large measure of cooperation) rather than division (and motives for corrosive competition).

The issue of influence also points in another direction. The architecture of NATO's future is essentially completed—although much work and many critical decisions still lie ahead in turning plans into reality; there are no fundamental strategic fault lines across the Atlantic; the European Union is growing in power, performance, wealth, and stature and is moving forward in key areas of both "widening" and "deepening"—with the latter including adoption of the Euro and the early steps in creating CFSP and ESDP. At the same time, an increasing share of the overall transatlantic relationship is shifting toward U.S. relations with the EU, not so much because of ESDP, but because (1) much of the strategic architecture is in place; yet (2) much of the long-term transatlantic economic relationship has not been defined. Thus, in the period ahead, it is likely that a larger part of adjustments in influence between the various parties to the transatlantic relationship will take place within areas that are EU-focused—and EU/U.S.–focused—as opposed to the classic strategic and political-military areas that have so much dominated the past. This is a further argument for breaking down traditional barriers between NATO and the EU, as well as within the U.S. and allied governments in terms of approaches to political-military and political-economic matters.

But none of these issues, fundamental to the long-term nature of transatlantic relationships, needs finally to be resolved now to draw a basic lesson about immediate developments in relations between NATO and EU/ESDP—and between the United States and its European partners in the field of defense and military affairs. Three points stand out:

- The ESDI-ESDP issue should not be dividing the United States and European allies in any fundamental way.

- "Getting ESDP right" should thus be high on the current transatlantic agenda, for political action by leaders on both sides of the Atlantic, designed to reduce this irritant to the degree possible and remove it as a complicating factor in addressing other transatlantic problems.

- There is no apparent reason why serious efforts by U.S. and EU leaders should not produce the desired results—a mutually reinforcing relationship between the European Union, acting through ESDP, and NATO that works for all and for overall security in the transatlantic region.

This monograph was completed before the tragic events of September 11, 2001—a second "date which will live in infamy." Less than a month later, as the campaign in Afghanistan was just beginning, it was not possible to predict with certainty the effects that the ensuing major changes in international politics will have on the role of the European Security and Defense Policy, or on its relationship to NATO. However, a number of developments and trends can already be discerned.

Following the attacks on the World Trade Center in New York and the Pentagon in Washington, the focus of attention in transatlantic security relations—including the role to be played within these relations by European institutions—turned first and foremost to NATO. On September 12, for the first time in NATO history, the North Atlantic Council

> agreed that if it is determined that this attack was directed from abroad against the United States, it shall be regarded as an action covered by Article 5 of the Washington Treaty, which states that an armed attack against one or more of the Allies in Europe or North America shall be considered an attack against them all.[1]

In fact, Article 5 of the Washington Treaty does not obligate any ally to do anything, except to decide to

---

[1] *NATO Press Release (2001)124,* September 12, 2001.

assist the Party or Parties so attacked by taking forthwith, individually and in concert with the other Parties, *such action as it deems necessary,* including the use of armed force, to restore and maintain the security of the North Atlantic area [emphasis added].[2]

This critical qualifier—"such action as it deems necessary"—was included in the treaty, at U.S. insistence, when it was negotiated in 1949 to preserve the right of the U.S. Congress to declare war, just as the United States also insisted on limiting the scope of the treaty's application to areas and forces in or abutting allied territories.[3] Indeed, in the period after September 11, the United States was not looking for the alliance as a whole to become engaged militarily against Osama bin Laden and his associates (although, in the longer-term prosecution of the war against international terrorism, such a request could materialize); and only the United Kingdom joined the United States in the first phase of the attacks on Afghanistan. Instead, the United States was primarily concerned about having the full *political* support of the allies—the true import of Article 5, from its inception—as well as some practical steps in the overall effort to

---

[2]Full text of Article 5 of the *Treaty of Washington,* April 4, 1949:

> The Parties agree that an armed attack against one or more of them in Europe or North America shall be considered an attack against them all and consequently they agree that, if such an armed attack occurs, each of them, in exercise of the right of individual or collective self-defence recognised by Article 51 of the Charter of the United Nations, will assist the Party or Parties so attacked by taking forthwith, individually and in concert with the other Parties, such action as it deems necessary, including the use of armed force, to restore and maintain the security of the North Atlantic area. Any such armed attack and all measures taken as a result thereof shall immediately be reported to the Security Council. Such measures shall be terminated when the Security Council has taken the measures necessary to restore and maintain international peace and security.

[3]Article 6 of the *Treaty of Washington*, April 4, 1949 (as amended):

> For the purpose of Article 5, an armed attack on one or more of the Parties is deemed to include an armed attack: on the territory of any of the Parties in Europe or North America, on . . . the territory of or on the Islands under the jurisdiction of any of the Parties in the North Atlantic area north of the Tropic of Cancer; on the forces, vessels, or aircraft of any of the Parties, when in or over these territories . . . or the Mediterranean Sea or the North Atlantic area north of the Tropic of Cancer.

counter terrorism.[4] The first tranche of U.S. requests to the full alliance was agreed upon by the North Atlantic Council on October 4, and it consisted mostly of indirect military assistance (e.g., overflight rights, movement of the Standing Naval Forces and Airborne Warning and Control aircraft); combined efforts at countering terrorism in nonmilitary ways; and, perhaps most important for this discussion of ESDP, the "backfill [i.e., replacement of U.S. military assets by] selected Allied assets in NATO's area of responsibility that are required to directly support operations against terrorism."[5] This

---

[4]As President George H.W. Bush had done in 1990–91 in *Desert Shield* and *Desert Storm*, the most important objective of the overall coalition—NATO and beyond—built for prosecuting the campaign against Osama bin Laden was political—to demonstrate to peoples of the Islamic world that (1) the United States was not acting alone and (2) it was also gaining the support of legitimate Islamic countries and leaders. In the Persian Gulf War, this political tactic was designed to counter Saddam Hussein's claim that he represented the "Arab Street" against the "Zionists and imperialists." Coalition with NATO countries also shows the American people that they are not alone in this effort, but have the support of critical allies for whom the United States has done so much and who share fundamental humane and democratic values.

[5]NATO Headquarters, October 4, 2001, *Statement to the Press by NATO Secretary General, Lord Robertson, on the North Atlantic Council Decision on Implementation of Article 5 of the Washington Treaty following the 11 September Attacks against the United States:*

> Following its decision to invoke Article 5 of the Washington Treaty in the wake of the 11 September attacks against the United States, the NATO Allies agreed today—at the request of the United States—to take eight measures, individually and collectively, to expand the options available in the campaign against terrorism. Specifically, they agreed to:
>
> - enhance intelligence sharing and co-operation, both bilaterally and in the appropriate NATO bodies, relating to the threats posed by terrorism and the actions to be taken against it;
>
> - provide, individually or collectively, as appropriate and according to their capabilities, assistance to Allies and other states which are or may be subject to increased terrorist threats as a result of their support for the campaign against terrorism;
>
> - take necessary measures to provide increased security for facilities of the United States and other Allies on their territory;
>
> - backfill selected Allied assets in NATO's area of responsibility that are required to directly support operations against terrorism;
>
> - provide blanket overflight clearances for the United States and other Allies' aircraft, in accordance with the necessary air traffic arrange-

"backfilling" most clearly related to some combination of the three NATO deployments in Bosnia, Kosovo, and Macedonia.

At the time of this writing, it was not clear what the full impact of this agreement by the NATO allies on backfilling would be—including how extensive it would be and for how long. In Washington, there was some pressure for the United States to remove all of its forces from these three NATO Balkan deployments, as had already been discussed earlier in the year, before September 11 and unrelated to issues of terrorism. Afterward, certainly the highest priority for the United States in terms of protecting its own security was to use whatever military resources it needed for the immediate effort against Osama bin Laden and other perpetrators of the September 11 crime. But should all U.S. military participation with other NATO allies and partners in the Balkans thus cease, even beyond the initial stages of the overall fight against international terrorism emanating from the Middle East? The implications of doing so would be clear: the emergence of an implicit—or even explicit—division of labor within the alliance, regarding which allies would do what. And, within the context of European NATO deployments and operations, there would be at least a technical breaking of the doctrine of shared risks (although in the Balkans, the risks have for some time been relatively minor). Thus, for the United States to turn all of its attention, in terms of mili-

---

ments and national procedures, for military flights related to operations against terrorism;

- provide access for the United States and other Allies to ports and airfields on the territory of NATO nations for operations against terrorism, including for refuelling, in accordance with national procedures.

The North Atlantic Council also agreed:

- that the Alliance is ready to deploy elements of its Standing Naval Forces to the Eastern Mediterranean in order to provide a NATO presence and demonstrate resolve; and

- that the Alliance is similarly ready to deploy elements of its NATO Airborne Early Warning force to support operations against terrorism.

Today's collective actions operationalise Article 5 of the Washington Treaty. These measures were requested by the United States following the determination that the 11 September attack was directed from abroad. These decisions clearly demonstrate the Allies' resolve and commitment to support and contribute to the U.S.-led fight against terrorism.

tary engagement in practical operations, away from Continental Europe and to the Middle East might have a strong pull; but it would not be without costs, and those would have to be measured, over time, in terms of the way in which the alliance sees itself as being "one for all and all for one."

Of course, there is a reverse side to this argument: With the invocation of Article 5 of the Washington Treaty, there ensued at least a moral and political obligation on the part of the other allies to assist the United States in dealing with the aggression to which it had been subjected. Even though this article was originally designed to engage the United States, morally and politically, in the defense of Europe if continental allies were attacked by the Soviet Union (during the cold war) or by someone else afterward (e.g., Turkey by Iraq), the Washington Treaty does apply to all the allies. It is a historical irony, perhaps, that it is the traditional, principal guarantor state for whom the guarantee was first invoked—although not at its specific request. The added irony, of course, is that the Washington Treaty originally envisioned that a collective response to aggression, at least prior to the initiation of nuclear hostilities, would be primarily *in situ,* that is, in Europe, presuming that a Soviet military attack would be against allied territory and forces in Europe. This was the burden of the subclause of Article 5: "to restore and maintain the security of the North Atlantic area." On this occasion, the initial military action (leaving aside what the locus of military action against international terrorism could be in the future) was some 7,000 miles from where the aggression was committed, and certainly beyond any definition of the territorial limits of Europe, or even of the extended territories embraced by the Partnership for Peace in the Caucasus and Central Asia. The Washington Treaty is silent on where the riposte should take place; it speaks only of the site of the initial aggression.

But even if there were no moral, political, and legalistic basis for allied support of the United States in responding to the aggression of September 11, there were compelling reasons for the Europeans to join with the United States. Indeed, the latter had little choice but to respond, not just to avenge those who were killed and wounded— and not just to try to reduce or end the scourge of international terrorism—but also to preserve its credibility as a major power. This issue was more existential than volitional: If the United States failed to take appropriate action in direct response to aggression against the homeland—and to do so successfully—then who in future would be willing to put full trust and confidence in U.S. pledges and engagements? Who would be confident that the United States could not be deterred from acting in its own or its allies' interests?

Furthermore, the European allies also had to consider several other factors:

- The assault was upon common values and, in fact, was a true "crime against humanity," in no small part because nationals of some 60 or more nations were killed.

- The United States had stood with the European allies in time of need for nearly a century, from 1917 onward, including the period following the cold war when its own strategic interests in Europe were less engaged than they had been before, and certainly less than those of virtually all European states; this included major U.S. responsibility for, and engagement in, peacemaking and peacekeeping in the Balkans.

- The allies also had to reckon that, at a time when the American people were so clearly hurting, failure to respond could have long-term consequences for the willingness of the United States to continue its basic commitments to European security, beyond actions based solely on simple U.S. self-interest; this could also affect other parts, including economic components, of the transatlantic relationship.

- They had to understand that, if they were not responsive to U.S. needs beyond Europe, then there could be a permanent shift of U.S. attention beyond the European continent. Earlier concerns in Europe that the United States might turn its attention more to Asia than to Europe may have caused Europeans to feel a sense of loss, based on what the allies could argue was U.S. misperception of its own interests. But no European could argue that the United States, in putting more emphasis on the Middle East than on Europe (at least for the time-being), was in any way misunderstanding its true interests, because the homeland had been attacked.

These arguments clearly conditioned the response of European governments to the United States after September 11. The response was also related to the "popular push" exerted by peoples of Europe who were, if anything, even more automatically sympathetic with what the United States was experiencing than were their governments. The sense of "we are all in this together" touched a critical nerve within these democratic societies.

But more was also involved. For some time, the alliance has been debating the range of its actions "outside of area," as described elsewhere in this work. The author has argued that the 1999 Kosovo conflict was, for the alliance, "not a bridge too far," in reference to the Arnhem offensive of 1944, but it was, to that point, certainly "the farthest bridge," in terms of where the alliance, collectively, was prepared to become engaged militarily. If Kosovo nearly split alliance cohesion, the argument ran, there would be little point in trying to get NATO to take concerted action any farther afield, except under extreme compulsion directly affecting the bulk or even all of the allies—as was true of the Iraqi invasion of Kuwait in 1991. This clear sense of limitation on the area where allies were prepared to act militarily, beyond the parameters of Articles 5 and 6 of the Washington Treaty, was obviously a major reason that the long-standing debate about alliance action beyond Europe was effectively shelved at the Washington NATO summit in April 1999, in favor of some very general language: "Alliance security must also take account of the global context," which could include "acts of terrorism."[6]

But with the events of September 11, the debate has reemerged—if so far only tacitly—and in a critical form. Even if the United States limits its requests for direct military support to a select few allies— such as British engagement beginning on October 7, and with

---

[6]NATO, *NATO Strategic Concept,* 1999 Washington NATO Summit, paragraph 24:

> Any armed attack on the territory of the Allies, from whatever direction, would be covered by Articles 5 and 6 of the Washington Treaty. However, Alliance security must also take account of the global context. Alliance security interests can be affected by other risks of a wider nature, including acts of terrorism, sabotage and organised crime, and by the disruption of the flow of vital resources. The uncontrolled movement of large numbers of people, particularly as a consequence of armed conflicts, can also pose problems for security and stability affecting the Alliance. Arrangements exist within the Alliance for consultation among the Allies under Article 4 of the Washington Treaty and, where appropriate, co-ordination of their efforts including their responses to risks of this kind.

pledges at that point of assistance by France, Germany, Italy, and Canada—as well as non-NATO ally Australia—the alliance perforce is now engaged "outside of area," meaning beyond Europe, because of the effects of international terrorism on the United States, if not also on other allied states.[7] The principle of the "outside of area" debate was thus settled by circumstances. The practical application of the outcome of this debate is yet to be decided, but there has been a decisive step forward. Or, if the European allies do not accept this point, the cohesion of the NATO Alliance would be in grave if not terminal trouble.

Nor should this shift in perspective have been entirely unexpected, except in terms of form and timing. In form, the argument for years was that an "outside of area" threat to the alliance (or to some of its members), to which the alliance would feel itself compelled to respond (i.e., Article 5 implications) would come in the form of weapons of mass destruction (WMD), not "terrorism" that did not employ such weapons. The World Trade Center and Pentagon attacks did not engage weapons of mass destruction, in terms of the physical destruction they caused, but rather were weapons of mass psychological disruption (WMPD), which obviously also have—and by their nature are designed to have—potent effects and consequences.[8] In terms of timing, some observers argued that a WMD

---

[7]This would be true even without the invocation of Article 5; obviously, its invocation has even greater meaning.

[8]In debate about so-called asymmetrical warfare, emphasis is generally put on WMD, because it is only these weapons that could cause an amount of physical destruction to offset—at least to some significant degree—the military advantages of the country being attacked. "Terrorism" is a form of asymmetrical warfare that is less about physical destruction (although with WMD that could be sizable) than about the psychological and political effects, within the classical definition. By that definition, terrorism is an act or acts of violence against noncombatants, at random and usually without warning, such that the broader class of noncombatants will identify with those against whom the violence has taken place and will be led by fear of further violence against themselves or other qualities they hold dear either to act *far out of proportion to the original attack* against themselves (or their societies) in ways the terrorists desire (e.g., self-protection out of proportion to risk but damaging to the local economy, or erosion of civil liberties) or to press governments to act in ways the terrorists desire (e.g., to change policies, release other terrorists from prison, or—including in the current situation—to stigmatize Islam in general and to strike militarily in ways that will cause significant civilian casualties). Both asymmetrical warfare with WMD (destruction) and without (WMPD—e.g., the kind of terrorism of September 11) are military weapons, since both are designed to cause political effects desired by the terrorists.

threat could emerge in the relatively near future; but no government was entirely persuaded of this proposition, and certainly the alliance as a whole was not (and, indeed, still is not). The new shift in timing is principally in regard not to WMD but to WMPD—which, as we have already seen, has galvanized the United States to a major response and commitment to a long-term campaign against international terrorism, even without the additional element—which could come—of WMD.

The principle of "outside of area" activity for the Atlantic Alliance, even beyond Europe, must now be conceded—in some form, if only in political support, steps like the eight that were agreed upon in the North Atlantic Council on October 4, and the military participation of "coalitions of the able and willing."

TOWARD A U.S./NATO–EUROPEAN UNION STRATEGIC PARTNERSHIP

However, the institutional expression of allies' being engaged beyond Europe are different from the trends prior to September 11. Notably, the military emphasis after September 11 has been totally on NATO, and the idea of using ESDP was not even discussed, at least not publicly—and, it can be argued, it would not have been considered seriously even if the Headline Goal Task Force where already in being. This emphasis is true primarily because of two factors: first, the kind of military effort most likely required to deal with terrorism (more of a "special forces" nature—perhaps backed up with precision airpower—rather than of a rapid reaction corps nature); and second, the need for coordinated, coherent action engaging the United States and its allies. To the extent that military action would be taken on a multilateral basis, involving an institution, that perforce would have to be NATO (assuming that the United States, in this case, would want to conduct its military operation through NATO which, as in the 1991 Persian Gulf War, it has so far not wanted to do and would be unlikely to do). Thus, in the first test of U.S.-

---

Terrorism (according to this classical, and most valid, definition—not just acts of insanity or zealotry without a political goal) is thus, like classic warfare, a "continuation of politics by other means."

European military-political cooperation beyond Europe, the primacy of NATO was asserted.

This lack of a direct role for ESDP might change during the longer-term campaign against international terrorism: There might be some situation in which the European Union would want to consider engaging the European rapid reaction forces on their own—a theoretical but perhaps not practical proposition.[9] By contrast, the U.S. pre-occupation both with Middle East–based international terrorism and with potential, perhaps unintended, consequences of the campaign (e.g., greater U.S. geopolitical responsibilities for the region or for particular countries—a sort of "East of Suez" orientation with attendant, semipermanent military deployments) could lead to a significant reduction in U.S. interest in the practical aspects of European security or in other regions nearby, such as North Africa. Then the EU's rapid reaction forces could gain greater saliency and importance. However, as noted above, that could produce the risk that the Europeans (ESDP) could begin to "backfill" for the United States in ways that would intrude into areas where NATO has classically been engaged, or where Partners for Peace—expecting strategic engagement by the United States—would see a lessening of U.S. interest. All implications of such a shift cannot be ascertained at this point; but this shift should not be entered into lightly.

However, there is already a way in which the European Union's efforts to create a foreign policy and security identity is engaged: It lies in the nexus between the two new entities—the Common Foreign and Security Policy and the European Security and Defense Policy. ESDP has not been involved in the post–September 11 crisis; but CFSP has been a centerpiece of EU action. In fact, it can be argued that a new strategic relationship between the United States and the European Union, such as has been promoted for some time by this author, has come into being since September 11.

This relationship began dramatically with the support for the United States shown by the EU, beginning immediately after September 11. Three days later, in the first-ever joint declaration by all the heads of

---

[9]Indeed, on September 14, the combined heads of state and government and heads of EU institutions said that: "We shall make the European Security and Defence Policy operational as soon as possible." See the next footnote, below.

state and government of the EU, plus the heads of all of its key institutions, the union took a strong stand. Most important, it declared:

> We will not, under any circumstances, allow those responsible to find refuge, wherever they may be. Those responsible for hiding, supporting or harbouring the perpetrators, organisers and sponsors of these acts will be held accountable. This assault on humanity struck at the heart of a close friend, a country with which the European Union is striving to build a better world. But these terrible terrorist attacks were also directed against us all, against open, democratic, multicultural and tolerant societies. We call on all countries that share these universal ideals and values to join together in the battle against terrorist acts perpetrated by faceless killers who claim the lives of innocent victims. Nothing can justify the utter disregard for ethical values and human rights. Global solidarity is at stake. Together, irrespective of our origins, race or religion, we must work tirelessly to find solutions to the conflicts that all too often serve as a pretext for savagery. We call on all countries to redouble their efforts in the fight against terrorism.[10]

---

[10]*Joint Declaration by the Heads of State and Government of the European Union, the President of the European Parliament, the President of the European Commission, and the High Representative for the Common Foreign and Security Policy,* September 14, 2001:

> In Europe, and around the world, the horrific terrorist attacks on the United States have shocked our citizens. As an expression of solidarity with the American people, Europe has declared 14 September a day of mourning. We invite all European citizens to observe, at noon, a three-minute silence to express our sincere and deepest sympathy for the victims and their families.
>
> On 12 September, the European Union condemned the perpetrators, organisers and sponsors of these terrorist attacks in the strongest possible terms. The European Union announced that it would make every possible effort to ensure that those responsible for these acts of savagery are brought to justice and punished.
>
> The US Administration and the American people can count on our complete solidarity and full cooperation to ensure that justice is done. We will not, under any circumstances, allow those responsible to find refuge, wherever they may be. Those responsible for hiding, supporting or harbouring the perpetrators, organisers and sponsors of these acts will be held accountable.
>
> This assault on humanity struck at the heart of a close friend, a country with which the European Union is striving to build a better world. But these terrible terrorist attacks were also directed against us all, against open, democratic, multicultural and tolerant societies. We call on all countries that

share these universal ideals and values to join together in the battle against terrorist acts perpetrated by faceless killers who claim the lives of innocent victims. Nothing can justify the utter disregard for ethical values and human rights. Global solidarity is at stake.

Together, irrespective of our origins, race or religion, we must work tirelessly to find solutions to the conflicts that all too often serve as a pretext for savagery.

We call on all countries to redouble their efforts in the fight against terrorism. This is essential for security of our citizens and the stability of our societies. International organisations, and the United Nations in particular, must make this an absolute priority. We shall act with determination and ambition to overcome any obstacles in our path. To eliminate this evil, the police and judicial authorities of all our countries must, in the coming days, intensify their efforts. International law makes it possible to hunt the perpetrators, organizers and instigators of terrorism wherever they are. It is not tolerable for any country to harbour terrorists.

These tragic events oblige us to take urgent decisions on how the European Union should respond to these challenges :

- The European Union must commit itself tirelessly to defend justice and democracy at a global level, to promote an international framework of security and prosperity for all countries, and to contribute towards the emergence of a strong, sustained and global action against terrorism.

- We shall continue to develop the Common Foreign and Security Policy with a view to ensuring that the Union is genuinely capable of speaking out clearly and doing so with one voice.

- We shall make the European Security and Defence Policy operational as soon as possible. We will make every effort to strengthen our intelligence efforts against terrorism.

- The European Union will accelerate the implementation of a genuine European judicial area, which will entail, among other things, the creation of a European warrant for arrest and extradition, in accordance with the Tampere conclusions, and the mutual recognition of legal decisions and verdicts.

Our citizens will not be intimidated. Our societies will continue to function undeterred. But today our thoughts are with the victims, their families and the American people.

Guy Verhofstadt, Tony Blair, Nicole Fontaine, Wolfgang Schüssel, Romano Prodi, Gerhard Schröder, José-Maria Aznar, Tarja Halonen, Poul Nyrup Rasmussen, Paavo Lipponen, Kostas Simitis, Antonio Guterres, Silvio Berlusconi, Jacques Chirac, Bertie Ahern, Lionel Jospin, Wim Kok, Göran Persson, Jean-Claude Juncker, Javier Solana.

In subsequent days, the EU took further practical steps in the fight against terrorism, including in the areas of attacking the flow of financing, cooperation in intelligence and through Interpol, and a host of other steps that added up to a robust package of cooperation.[11]

---

[11]See, for instance (all from *EU News* [Delegation of the European Commission, Washington, D.C.]), "EU Commission Calls for Common Instruments to Tackle Terrorism," September 19, 2001; "European Union Steps up Fight Against Terrorism: The EU Council of Justice and Home Affairs Ministers," September 20, 2001; and "EU Steps up Fight Against Financing of International Terrorism," October 3, 2001.

"US-EU Ministerial Statement on Combating Terrorism," *EU News* (Delegation of the European Commission, Washington, D.C.), September 20, 2001:

> In the coming days, weeks and months, the United States and the European Union will work in partnership in a broad coalition to combat the evil of terrorism. We will act jointly to expand and improve this cooperation worldwide. Those responsible for the recent attacks must be tracked down and held to account. We will mount a comprehensive, systematic and sustained effort to eliminate international terrorism—its leaders, its actors, its networks. Those responsible for aiding, supporting or harboring the perpetrators, organizers and sponsors of these acts will be held accountable. Given the events of September 11, 2001 it is imperative that we continue to develop practical measures to prevent terrorists from operating.
>
> Our resolve is a reflection of the strength of the U.S.-EU relationship, our shared values, and our determination to address together the new challenges we face. The nature of our democratic societies makes it imperative to protect our citizens from terrorist acts, while at the same time protecting their individual liberties, due process, and the rule of law. The U.S. and the EU are committed to enhancing security measures, legislation and enforcement. We will work together to encourage greater cooperation in international fora and wider implementation of international instruments. We will also cooperate in global efforts to bring to justice perpetrators of past attacks and to eliminate the ability of terrorists to plan and carry out future atrocities. We have agreed today that the United States and the EU will vigorously pursue cooperation in the following areas in order to reduce vulnerabilities in our societies:
>
> - Aviation and other transport security
> - Police and judicial cooperation, including extradition
> - Denial of financing of terrorism, including financial sanctions
> - Denial of other means of support to terrorists
> - Export control and nonproliferation
> - Border controls, including visa and document security issues

While this one area of cooperation—on international terrorism, essentially focused on the Middle East—is not a sufficient basis on which to make broad generalizations, at least in this one area there is developing something of a strategic partnership between the EU and NATO (and, perhaps more pertinently, the EU and the United States), but this is through the CFSP, not ESDP. But, in terms of the EU's competence and efforts to build its institutions, there is nothing wrong with this: Indeed, from NATO's point of view, over the long term, it could be preferable to having to contend with competition from ESDP. The relationship with CFSP (supplementing but not replacing bilateral U.S. cooperation with countries such as the U.K. and France) is a natural fit; and it also has the virtue of helping to make up for a natural defect in NATO's development, discussed earlier, which is its lack of a true capacity for crisis management, other than specific tasks from time to time delegated to the secretary general, as in Macedonia during 2001. If ESDP goes into the deep freeze for a time, that would not be a bad thing from NATO's perspective; it would put aside the vexatious issues of competitive operational planning; it would restore primacy to NATO on issues of significant importance to allies; and it would help to ensure that the United States would see the relationship with the EU in this area as a matter of cooperation, compatibility, and complementarity, rather than competition. Of course, such an outcome might not last very long, or it may not apply to other aspects of foreign policy and security— since the terrorism issue, while important, is not the be-all and end-all of concerns in international relations, for either the United States or its European allies and partners.

There are some other preliminary lessons of September 11 for NATO's relations with the European Union, in regard to CFSP/ESDP, that are worth noting:

- There is now a greater premium on integrating different aspects of policy between the European Union and the United States (to the degree possible also embracing NATO as an institution, as in some of the tasks agreed upon by the North Atlantic Council on

    - Law enforcement access to information and exchange of electronic data.

October 4) including military, political/diplomatic, intelligence, finance, and judicial/police.

- Regarding the new emphasis on combating international terrorism and concomitant concerns about the capacity for different allies to act militarily beyond Europe, to at least some degree, there will be an added premium, as well, on the capacity of the allied militaries to be interoperable. This will be particularly true with regard to C³ISR, but certainly not limited to it.

- This lesson about interoperability also applies to the development of relations between defense and other security industries on both sides of the Atlantic; for one thing, the issue of transfers of high technology from the United States to allies now urgently needs to be resolved.

- In terms of being able to manage a complex and effective campaign against international terrorism, individual European allies will need to keep up relevant spending, although much of this might not be directly for the military services; comprehensive security budgeting will be increasingly important—a lesson for the United States, as well.

- As relationships develop among the various institutions—EU (CFSP/ESDP), NATO, and bilaterally across the Atlantic—there will be considerable value in developing a common locus for counterterrorism planning and coordination. This could consist of a permanent coordinating staff and council involving both the EU and NATO, and including all the relevant parts of governments. Given the special need for U.S. leadership, direct engagement of the U.S. National Security Council process with this new Transatlantic Counter-Terrorism Coordinating Council could pay major dividends.

THE LONGER PERSPECTIVE

Following the end of Phase 1—the campaign against Osama bin Laden, al-Qaeda, other perpetrators of the September 11 crimes, and, by extension, the Taliban regime in Afghanistan—the nature of relations between the United States and its European allies and partners will necessarily shift. The United States was given almost *carte blanche* after September 11—although European leaders made clear that their support for U.S. policy and actions was designed, in part, to gain themselves a "seat at the table" in determining future U.S. counterterrorism policy. Sustaining a coalition, even including Europeans, will be much more complex later on—as indeed the United States has already recognized.[12]

Several other factors, still developing, will also be important. They include the following:

- Different definitions of the terrorist "threat"—what is it and against whom is it directed. Is this indeed a "war" that engages all the allies in common?

- Will individual European allies seek U.S. support for a definition of international terrorism that includes their own preoccupations—e.g., the Provisional IRA and Basque separatist terrorism?

- When will the requirement of Article 5 be satisfied ("to restore and maintain the security of the North Atlantic area"), and how will that be decided?

- What, in fact, will be the common allied definition of "victory"?

- Will the United States and its allies agree on the importance of trying to reduce the appeal of terrorists within their societies, regions, and cultures? This relates to the doctrine of Mao Zedong: creating a "sea for the [terrorist] fish to swim in," and the role of trying to "dry up" that sea? For the Europeans, most important is consistent, even-handed, and deeply engaged U.S. leadership in trying to resolve the Arab-Israeli conflict.

- To what extent will the United States see the conflict against international terrorism as something to be centrally directed and controlled from Washington, as opposed to a genuine "multilateral" effort?

---

[12]See Donald H. Rumsfeld, *The New York Times*, September 27, 2001:

> This war will not be waged by a grand alliance united for the single purpose of defeating an axis of hostile powers. Instead, it will involve floating coalitions of countries, which may change and evolve. Countries will have different roles and contribute in different ways. Some will help us publicly, while others, because of their circumstances, may help us privately and secretly. In this war, the mission will define the coalition—not the other way around.

- What will be the agreed upon importance within the alliance of acting against WMD—especially nuclear weapons and including such issues as arms control, the Anti-Ballistic Missile Treaty, and ballistic missile defenses—and what strategies, broadly grouped into preventative, deterrent, and protectionist, could be agreed upon to counter proliferation?

- To what extent will the United States be able to count on continuing European support? Will it be past the point when Europeans, in the main are "satisfied" that efforts against international terrorism have been largely successful, as the Europeans press the United States to be "internationalist" in its overall outlook on international engagement (an extension of debates current during the latter Clinton and George W. Bush administrations prior to September 11)?

- To what extent will the campaign against international terrorism affect other aspects of the Atlantic Alliance, including the roles of NATO and the EU (CFSP and ESDP), other foreign policy and national security interests, and the whole corpus of transatlantic relations?

This last question may prove to be the most significant.